What Therapists Learn about Themselves and How They Learn It: Autognosis

What Therapists Learn about Themselves and How They Learn It: Autognosis

Edited by

EDWARD MESSNER, M.D.
JAMES E. GROVES, M.D.
JONATHAN H. SCHWARTZ, M.D.

JASON ARONSON INC.
Northvale, New Jersey
London

THE MASTER WORK SERIES, 1994

ISBN: 1-56821-188-0
Library of Congress Catalog Card Number: 93-74196

Manufactured in the United States of America. Jason Aronson Inc. offers books and cassettes. For information and catalog write to Jason Aronson Inc., 230 Livingston Street, Northvale, New Jersey 07647.

Contributors

Ellen Andrews, M.D.
Private Practice of Psychiatry and Neurology; Attending Physician, Moore Regional Hospital, Pinehurst, North Carolina

Marie Armentano, M.D.
Assistant in Psychiatry, Massachusetts General Hospital; Instructor in Psychiatry, Harvard Medical School, Boston, Massachusetts

Arthur J. Barsky III, M.D.
Assistant Professor of Psychiatry, Harvard Medical School; Director, Primary Care Psychiatric Unit, Massachusetts General Hospital, Boston, Massachusetts

Andrew Brotman, M.D.
Director, Social and Community Psychiatry, Department of Psychiatry, Massachusetts General Hospital; Assistant Professor of Psychiatry, Harvard Medical School, Boston, Massachusetts

John T. Carr, M.D.
Clinical Director, Newport Community Health Center, Newport, Rhode Island

Joseph A. Deltito, M.D.
Chief, Anxiety and Depression Clinic, Assistant Professor of Psychiatry, Cornell University Medical College, New York, New York; Visiting Professor of Psychiatry and Psychopharmacology, University of Pisa, Pisa, Italy

Louise Dierker, M.D., M.P.H.
Member, Boston Psychoanalytic Society; Adjunct Assistant Professor of Psychiatry, Dartmouth Medical School, Hanover, New Hampshire; Private Practice of Psychoanalysis, New Hampshire and Vermont

Paul Hamburg, M.D.
Clinical Instructor in Psychiatry, Harvard Medical School; Staff Psychiatrist, Eating Disorders Unit, Massachusetts General Hospital, Boston, Massachusetts

Michael S. Jellinek, M.D.
Director, Outpatient Psychiatry and Chief, Child Psychiatry Service, Massachusetts General Hospital; Associate Professor of Psychiatry (Pediatrics), Harvard Medical School, Boston, Massachusetts

Arthur Kleinman, M.D.
Professor of Medical Anthropology, Department of Social Medicine, Harvard Medical School and Department of Anthropology, Faculty of Arts and Sciences, Harvard University; Professor of Psychiatry, Harvard Medical School and Cambridge Hospital; Curator of Medical Anthropology in The Peabody Museum of Archaeology and Ethnology, Harvard University, Cambridge, Massachusetts

Stephen Kleinman, M.D.
Clinical Instructor in Psychiatry, Harvard Medical School; Clinical Associate, Massachusetts General Hospital; Medical Director, Mental Health, North End Health Center, Boston, Massachusetts

Bruce Lydiard, Ph.D., M.D.
Associate Professor, Director, Psychopharmacology Unit, Medical Director, Anxiety Disorders Research Program, Department of Psychiatry and Behavioral Sciences, Medical University of South Carolina, Charleston, South Carolina

Theo C. Manschreck, M.D.
Associate Professor of Psychiatry, Associate Psychiatrist, Massachusetts General Hospital; Clinical Director, Erich Lindemann Mental Health Center, Boston, Massachusetts

Alexander L. Miller, M.D.
Professor of Psychiatry and Pharmacology, University of Texas Health Science Center at San Antonio; Chief, Psychiatry Service, Audie L. Murphy Memorial Veterans' Hospital, San Antonio, Texas

Mark Harris Pollack, M.D.
Assistant Professor of Psychiatry, Harvard Medical School; Staff Psychiatrist, Clinical Psychopharmacology Unit, Massachusetts General Hospital, Boston, Massachusetts

Richard C. Rice, M.D.
Private Practice of Psychiatry, Northampton, Massachusetts

Joel F. Rubenstein, M.D.
Private Practice, Harris Street Associates, Newburyport, Massachusetts

Gary Sachs, M.D.
Assistant Psychiatrist, Clinical Psychopharmacology Unit, Department of Psychiatry, Massachusetts General Hospital; Instructor in Psychiatry, Harvard Medical School, Boston, Massachusetts

Rege Stewart, M.D.
Associate Professor of Psychiatry, University of Texas Southwestern Medical School; Director of Psychiatric Outpatient Clinics, Parkland Hospital, Dallas, Texas

Paul Summergrad, M.D.
Director, Inpatient Psychiatry Service, Massachusetts General Hospital; Instructor in Psychiatry, Harvard Medical School, Boston, Massachusetts

Albert V. Vogel, M.D.
Assistant Professor, Department of Psychiatry, University of New Mexico School of Medicine, Albuquerque, New Mexico

Scott N. Wilson, M.D.
Medical Director, Revere Community Counselling Center; Assistant in Psychiatry, Massachusetts General Hospital; Clinical Instructor in Psychiatry, Harvard Medical School, Boston, Massachusetts

Sidney Zisook, M.D.
Professor of Psychiatry, Director of Outpatient Research and Training, University of California, San Diego, California

Contents

Introduction

This book explores the self-help experiences of psychiatrists. It consists of personal accounts by psychiatrists who participated in the Autognosis Seminar at the Massachusetts General Hospital and reveals something of what these psychiatrists learned about themselves and how they learned it. Readers who are not psychiatrists may find these revelations instructive and useful for acquiring techniques and enhancing useful knowledge of themselves.

The primary objective in designing the Autognosis Seminar was protection of the psychiatric trainee. In the late 1960s, I became increasingly concerned about the stresses on psychiatric residents, especially in their first year of training. This concern arose from my experience as a clinical supervisor and instructor.

The emotional stresses placed on psychiatrists in general, and trainees in particular, are often intense. Back then several resources were available for the protection of psychiatric residents. These included psychoanalysis, psychotherapy, and some of the more supportive supervisory experiences. Another source of protection (but often a source of stress as well) was the training group, the "T group."

In addition to their own inherent personal strength, the residents gained comfort and protection from their colleagues, their spouses, and from their families. They could derive cognitive reinforcement from the books and papers that they read, from the information that they received from their academic instruction in residency, and from some of the clinical discussions and conferences.

But each of these resources had its own shortcomings. Psychoanalysis was relatively unavailable, and by its very nature was slow in producing its effects. Psychotherapy was a bit faster but usually focused on personal problems more than on the day-to-day professional stresses to which the resident was exposed. The various cognitive sources — reading, lectures, seminars — could fortify the intellectual side of the experience, but often did not alleviate the specific emotional stresses that the resident had to confront in the course of daily clinical responsibilities.

What seemed to be needed was a seminar that would focus directly and specifically on the subjective experiences of the resident. The topic of "countertransference" came to mind as a suitable vehicle for such a seminar. Accordingly, I organized a seminar on countertransference, which was given in the academic year 1968 to 1969. Countertransference is a term that came from psychoanalysis, and it refers to experiences of the therapist in response to the patients with whom he or she has therapeutic contact.

This seminar focused on papers from the classic psychoanalytic literature and led to some discussion of the clinical experiences of residents. It soon became clear that countertransference was too narrow a subject to accomplish the protective function that I had envisioned. Since it dealt only with the experiences that residents had with their patients, it left out a variety of other common and sometimes extremely stressful experiences. Examples were interactions with the hospital bureaucracy and relationships with other professionals in the field of psychiatry or with those in other medical fields. The subject omitted current stresses related to the clinician's family.

These omissions soon became evident in seminar discussions. At times the residents drifted off to mention some of the problems they were having with their own senses of identity as psychiatrists and their confrontations with residents in their own and other disciplines. They mentioned some of the daily ethical dilemmas with which they had to struggle, for example, how it feels to try to find help for a desperately ill patient who is unable to pay for psychiatric care.

A broader seminar was indicated. The following year the title was changed to *Autognosis,* and the subject matter grew to cover the subjective experiences of the first year resident in all professional capacities. Papers were chosen from the literature on countertransference and self-analysis, including papers on subjects that extended beyond the one-to-one clinical experience. These included papers on subjective experiences of people in education, and community mental health, and responses to victims of persecution.

In subsequent years, an additional feature enriched the seminar format. Residents gave individual presentations consisting of papers that were not on the assigned reading list or presentations of clinical experiences of their own. They also presented something about themselves if they wished: information or discussion of what they had learned about themselves and how they had learned it.

It was this last category of presentations that was most impressive. Some were moving and tremendously instructive, not only to the residents but to me as well. They were highly varied in their sources. A few of the residents presented material from their own personal journals and diaries, sometimes material that followed a particular theme. One example was how the resident chose the field of medicine. Another theme was how the resident chose psychiatry as a specialty. Other presentations related to their reactions to literature. One of the residents had read *Moby Dick* at three different phases of his life and told how each reading affected his understanding of himself.

Over the years, it has been a great privilege for me to hear those presentations and to participate in their discussions, so it seemed that it might be of value to others as well. This book is an attempt to fulfill that expectation.

Although the book does not permit the interactive participation that one can have in a seminar, it may provide the reader with some examples. It illustrates some of the approaches of carefully selected, highly motivated doctors engaged in learning about themselves. My comments preceding and following each essay call attention to themes and ideas that might have been discussed in the seminar.

Originally, the purpose of the seminar was to protect the resident against the stresses of residency training, and to reduce the severity and frequency of depression, anxiety, alcoholism, marital disruption, and other symptoms of emotional stress. But the work of the seminar, and the processes that it seemed to catalyze, implied we could go beyond protection from psychopathology. We could proceed toward increased strength, toward the development of increased emotional strength through the discussions and the methods we were developing.

The early studies and papers on countertransference focused on its impediments to psychoanalysis and psychotherapy, but eventually, countertransference emerged as a source of insight. Similarly, in the seminar, we attempted to prevent impediments to training, but we began to recognize that new insights and reinforcements of training could be developed through autognosis. We came to feel that not only could the resident become stronger by knowing more about inner workings, but he or she could also become a more effective diagnostician and a more effective therapist.

As the leader of this seminar over the years, I came to believe that a number of principles are relevant to effective teaching of autognosis.

Readers who contemplate development of such a seminar or who want more knowledge of its infrastructure may find these ideas useful.

The first of these is the recognition that it can be done. In the history of psychoanalysis, some have claimed that the only really useful self-knowledge is derived from undergoing classical psychoanalysis. Others widened the notion to include psychodynamic psychotherapy as a possible source of self-knowledge on the part of clinicians. My experience with the seminar suggests that clinically useful self-knowledge can be derived from conscientious and systematic cultivation of the emotional proprioception that is available to almost all human beings.

Proprioception, neurologically speaking, is position sense, a sense as necessary as hearing or sight. We can become aware of whether we are experiencing a fullness in the abdomen, pressure of the chair against our back; we can even tell the position of our hands or feet without looking at them. Without it, we cannot maintain our posture.

Similarly, when our attention is called to it, we can become aware, most of us, of whether we are feeling sad, calm, stimulated, annoyed, or tired. Even subtler subjective states may be recognizable. The basic "emotional proprioception" that is available to most human beings can be expanded and cultivated systematically in the same conscientious manner in which professionals learn their disciplines and enhance their skills.

A second principle of teaching relevant to the seminar is the teaching-learning contract. This means an explicit agreement between the instructor and the seminar participants about the goals, methods, and format of the seminar. Included in this is a special feature, confidentiality. It is crucial for the participants in such a seminar to agree that the specific content of what is discussed will remain confidential among the participants. Such an agreement increases the freedom to reveal private feelings and ideas.

Provision of a cognitive framework is another principle. The papers on the reading list are valuable, but they also serve as a point of orientation and as an intellectual refuge. The opportunity to discuss the authors' experiences and points of view allows the participant to engage in the subject without necessarily revealing anything until, and unless, he or she is ready.

A fourth principle is active participation. The requirement of an individual presentation in the second half of the seminar year seems to provide an enhancement to learning this subject. Active participation in learning clinically related subject matter tends to be more effective than passive receptivity.

A fifth process that adds to the seminar learning experience is self-revelation by the instructor. Ever since the early days, I offered some of my own experiences along with those of the residents in the course of the discussions. It is difficult to assess how useful or important this was, but over the years a number of the residents remarked that it was helpful to them to hear about the experiences of a senior practitioner.

Not too long ago, a colleague surprised me by recalling something from the seminar when he was a resident more than a decade ago. He said, "I remember a time when you were telling us about an experience when you were analyzing. There was this big borderline guy, and you were frightened of him. Sometimes he would rage at you in a way that was just about overwhelming. Your association was to a training plane in the Air Force, where the pilot and you were sitting in tandem. That was basically the position you were in with respect to the patient. I don't remember what the bottom line on that was, but I do recall that somehow it gave you sustenance."

When he brought up this anecdote, I remembered it vividly. The association that I had had was to a situation in which I was flying the plane, and the instructor pilot who was up front — as a test — switched off the engine. We were flying within a couple of miles of the North Korean line, near the Demilitarized Zone. I not only had the problem of keeping the plane from stalling and crashing, but also to keep it from wandering over North Korean air space, where we would certainly have been shot down. The "bottom line," as he put it, was that it came out all right.

All of my flight training experiences came out all right, even though there was danger. Neither of us died. I learned from that training experience in the airplane and became more confident. The same thing happened in the analysis of the patient.

In the plane, I found I had the skill to deal with the situation as a result of prior instruction. The same held true of the analytic situation. In addition, I had great confidence in the instructor pilot. I knew that I could trust him. That was the key in the analytic situation. As an analyst, I knew that I could, deep down, trust this analysand, even though he was at times overcome by rage. I knew that I was actually safe with him, that he would not harm me. He knew that we were both in it together. As in the airplane, if one of us got killed, probably both of us would have been destroyed.

THE SCOPE OF AUTOGNOSIS

Countertransference refers to the subjective response of the clinician to the analysand, the patient. Self-analysis deals with what analysts or people who have been psychoanalyzed learn about themselves, and how they learn it.

Autognosis covers a spectrum of responses to colleagues, patients, other mental health professionals of various disciplines, as well as responses to the bureaucracy, the medical delivery system, and other experiences that the clinician encounters in a professional role.

Autognosis has several dimensions. It is a body of knowledge that an individual develops about the self and its subjectivity. It includes the methods and processes by which he or she acquires this knowledge. It also includes the methods by which this knowledge of the self can be applied to enhance personal development and vigor and to solve professional problems.

Autognosis does not require adherence to any psychological school or point of view. It does not depend on free association, but can make use of it. It does not even depend on the concept of the dynamic unconscious, although in my experience such a concept can be a meaningful addition to one's autognostic repertoire.

Autognosis involves observation, development of a set of procedures for increasing one's knowledge and understanding, and application of that understanding in a constructive way. It is a sweeping spectrum of internal activities. Countertransference is one segment of that spectrum, and self-analysis is another segment. In autognosis we have to learn to recognize our responses and find ways of classifying them in order to apply them most usefully.

The applications are directed not only to prevent damage to ourselves but also to prevent damage to the patient in a clinical situation. They are also devoted to adding to our own strengths and emotional vitality and to enhancing the professional situations to which we apply ourselves.

It is artificial to try to separate the professional from the personal. Recognizing this artificial boundary in the seminar, we focus as much as we can on the professional aspect of our experience rather than the personal. But the boundary is highly permeable, and we may use one domain to enrich the other.

Practitioners of the medical specialty of psychiatry may find familiar experiences among these essays. Other members of the helping professions, especially those related to mental health, also may find much that is recognizable. Readers with other occupations may have to translate to the language of their own experience to achieve a degree of identification with these authors. Perhaps the key to such reframing is to view the patient as a person toward whom one has a significant social or personal duty. With that redefinition, the experiences described here might more meaningfully serve as models or guides.

The authors and the editors hope that the disclosures that follow will help invigorate the reader's own inward search.

Introduction to 'LOVING PATIENTS'

Many patients feel attracted to their therapists. Those feelings may be romantic, dependent, friendly, affectionately yearning, or possessive. Sometimes the attraction is strongly sexual in nature.

The basis for such attraction is partly realistic and partly emanates from the emotional background of the individual patient. On a realistic basis, psychotherapists, if they are acting in a professional manner, will be respectful, attentive, and helpful. Appropriate behavior for a physician is to be knowledgeable and calm, as well as interested in the well-being and improvement of the patient. This kind of behavior by itself is often attractive to the patient. It often contrasts markedly to many current or past social and personal relationships.

Many patients come to psychotherapy because they have suffered from troubling relationships. They may have experienced abuse or exploitation in their families, or they may have endured trauma outside. Some patients may have developed personality traits that provoke unfavorable responses in other people, or they may have had symptoms that interfered with satisfying interactions with others. Consequently, many patients have a strong desire for a more satisfying personal experience when they enter psychotherapy. They may generate a wish, either conscious or otherwise, to have the therapist fulfill some of their unsatisfied desires.

At times, psychotherapists experience reciprocating emotions and develop strong personal desires toward the patient. This can be a source of agonizing conflict within the therapist because he or she is required by his professional duty to maintain a helpful and relatively objective stance toward the patient. The clinician is duty-bound to protect and to help the patient and not to use the patient to satisfy personal desires. Emotional exploitation of patients violates the code of medical ethics. And, of course, vulnerability to such conflict and its attendant distress tends to be greater in relatively inexperienced clinicians.

Chapter 1

LOVING PATIENTS:
Struggles of a First Year
Psychiatric Resident

Andrew Brotman, M.D.

Sometimes, "transference" can't explain everything.

You're sitting in an office with an attractive young woman as you have been doing two hours a week for the last year. She's telling you how deeply she cares about you, how you know her better than anyone else ever has. She has never been as honest with anyone else and has been able to say whatever she feels. For the last few months, she has been feeling real emotion after years of avoiding closeness.

There is no one like you among her social contacts, and she is getting sick of going out with men who just want to get into her pants and then go home to their wives. She doesn't know very much about your outside life, but on the basis of your talks she finds you warm, honest, and caring.

She sometimes dreams of meeting you on the street and striking up a conversation. She imagines you ask her out to dinner, and the two of you have a good time, talk about mutual interests, have a few drinks. After dinner—who knows? She tells you she is certain that if you were free of professional constraints you would want to be with her.

1

Actually the whole idea sounds pretty damn good to you, but you nod stiffly, noncommittal.

So you go on with your day and try to figure out how you are going to interpret the obvious overidealizing positive transference. You heard those fancy words from your senior supervisor when you started training. (He's the guy who never showed you any facial expression for three months until you asked him if he thought you were doing all right or if he thought you were a total asshole. He smiled faintly and said you weren't a total asshole.) Thanks, pal.

Anyway, that overidealized transference meant that she thinks you are God's gift to the world (no, your relationship with your mother isn't transference) when in reality she doesn't know if you spend your free time stealing old ladies' handbags.

So you try and understand the "transference" and decide her impulses must be repetitions of feelings she has had toward significant others in early childhood. Perhaps her fantasies about her father are unconsciously displaced onto you. You think about clever interpretations you might lay on her so that therapy can proceed without this "resistance."

Sometimes, you find yourself dreaming about her, or fantasizing about her while you're watching a baseball game. You wonder if you would have asked her out if you had met her in a Chinese cooking class rather than in a doctor's office. You know where she hangs out after work, and you avoid those places. However, when you have to be in that neighborhood you may quickly walk by her favorite haunt and glance through the window. If you're with your girlfriend at the time, you might stop holding hands momentarily, pretending to wipe something from your eye with the index finger of that particular hand.

You somehow wouldn't want your patient to see that you were with "another woman." It would complicate the therapeutic process. Do you just want to keep the sexual tension alive so things stay interesting? Will she disintegrate if she finds out that her main man has a life outside the office? You know that she's got serious difficulties, but you like her and feel things could change for her if you had a different type of relationship. Or are those just rescue fantasies?

So you put it out of your mind, go to an afternoon movie, and think that it all must be countertransference. Clearly, the irrational feelings you're having will get in the way of the therapeutic process. You must monitor them and create mysterious internal devices so that you can perform therapeutically. At first you might keep it all to yourself, not wanting to share with your colleagues and supervisors your perverted inner life. You might run it by your own shrink, but what the hell would he know anyway. He's a middle-aged training analyst who smokes a pipe, occasionally grunts, and hasn't felt a "rising tide" of emotion in years. Or so you think. You're afraid to ask, thinking maybe your psychopathology is much more serious than you believed.

She's been pretty angry with you over the last few weeks. She's thinking of quitting therapy and says it's all been a sham. She just got finished telling you how important you were to her, and now she's saying that it's all been one-sided. You invited her to share intimate feelings in a therapeutic relationship, but she thinks it's a one-way street: While she is spilling her guts, you hide behind a cloak of personal mystery and "how can we understand this together" stuff. And when she's getting somewhere you glance at your watch and say time is up. Sure it's a two-way street — you're driving a Mack truck and she's on a minibike.

Listen asshole — she has strong feelings for you but you don't get it. She even has to pay to be with you — pretty pathetic when you have to pay to be with the person who is most important in your life. You're just a doctor doing a job that you have to do — you don't really care about her "as a person." You don't care.

Bullshit you don't care. You want to grab her by the shoulders, shake her and say "of course I care, you idiot! Why else do you think I put up with your shit?" You carefully consider that option and decide it wouldn't really be therapeutic, so how do you handle it? Perhaps it's all a recapitulation of the way she makes everyone feel on the outside. Or perhaps, at this time in her life you happen to be an appropriate choice if it were not for the professional relationship. You're a nice guy, together enough, a doctor, make a good living, will probably be a good family man. So what should you do with her feelings? How much of this is transference and how much of it is "real?" If you interpret the real relationship as transference, then it appears you don't care. If you acknowledge aspects of the real relationship, you wonder if you'll remain therapeutic. You contemplate going to law school, but you realize that in the psychotherapy game there's no safe place to hide. You put on your most impassive supervisor's face, reach for your pipe, and start to address the issue. Then you remember that you don't smoke.

While you're lying awake that night, you're thinking that you've been sucked in and seduced by the patient: You're both so narcissistic that you're feeding off each other's pathology. Maybe you're believing that the positive feelings are directed toward you as a person when it wouldn't matter if there was a mannequin sitting in your chair. Or maybe it really is all transference and you're too inexperienced to figure it out. These explanations are possible but it doesn't explain everything that's going on. She's making a *not* inappropriate choice of men but is angered by the reality. You can't interpret that away—you've got to talk about it.

Much easier said than done, buddy boy. By inviting her to talk about her fantasies and feelings, you both get a handle on the reality of the situation and try to cope with the frustrations involved. To ignore it is a mistake and can lead to acting out by the patient. But how do you control the flushing, palpitations, and sweating when you get into this stuff? Your voice quavers, you get a little dizzy, and if things get really bad you dredge up a visual image of your old high school baseball coach. You hated that guy, and his image straightens you out every time. You've got to do everything you can to tolerate the emotions in the room.

So there you are in your office with a patient who has problems, but you are certain that some aspects of her relationship with you is not transference. You're swimming in fantasy, desire, and confusion trying to find some principle or strategy to keep you afloat. Most of the time you've got things under control, but when you're uncertain enough to call on the coach for help, you need some guidelines.

First, psychotherapy is a serious business that is conducted between a patient and a therapist and cannot take place between friends, lovers, or relatives. It is a professional relationship no matter how emotionally charged it becomes. Presumably, this patient finds it much safer to discuss her innermost feelings if it is clear that the relationship is a professional one. Courtly behavior may take place in the context of a therapeutic relationship, and that's perfectly all right as long as the patient knows that you are ultimately setting limits. If you are seductive and lead the patient to believe that something else can develop, she may very well tailor the content of her sessions to try and please you, in order to make her a more desirable partner in your eyes. You could be lulled into thinking how well things are going in the therapy until you are unpleasantly surprised. You'll still be able to fantasize about each other, modeling can take place, you can become an ideal model, and you can effectively use all that material as long as the real relationship is clarified.

It's got to be clarified in your head too, kiddo. Let's say you're new in this business, and you're setting up shop in a new part of the country. You're not involved in a significant romantic relationship right now, and you don't know too many people in town. You work 12 hours a day, come home to an empty apartment, pop a TV dinner in the oven, watch the news, and have a beer. You go to bed early, get up the next day, and do the same thing. You try to be empathic and tolerate as much emotion from patients as you can. By the end of the week, you've given everything you've got, and they might as well hang you up in a deli window for the weekend. You went in to this job thinking about how stimulating it is, how intimate things get with your patient, how satisfying it is to always be dealing with people. That may be true, but if you think you can substitute it for a satisfying personal life, you better get help yourself. You need to get your emotional gratification somewhere else, or at least have insight so that you don't mess up the patient's mind. Fantasize all you want, but don't overgratify, withhold, or use the patient to complete your own life. Sure, you can learn from her but you've got to stay therapeutic. Mind games are almost as destructive as physical transgressions, and they're a lot harder to figure out.

Seeking romantic partners who are unavailable is a pattern that is not uncommon and can be explored. I'm talking about her, bozo.

But if it applies to you too, you might as well take a look at it. You are frequently inviting love to develop between yourself and your patient — particularly for those patients who come to you complaining of an inability to love. When they start to feel loving impulses, the "real" relationship and the "transference" get all tangled up. To a certain extent it is unfair, insofar as this love would probably not develop between the two of you in any sphere outside of the office. You can't interpret it away, or pretend it isn't there, but you can clarify the distortions and manipulations taking place in the room and see if they are the same phenomena that have resulted in unsatisfactory relationships for the patient in the past. You're working just as hard as she is, and that's what you were hired for. It's not unfair; it's just a job that requires a knowledge of yourself, a reasonably satisfying personal life, the ability to tolerate affect, a good observing eye, and a familiarity with theory. Nothing to it.

You know, situations like this aren't morally or ethically right or wrong. They exist and have to be dealt with. There are patients out there you can't stand and continue to treat out of duty. The common thread is that their relationship with you is the forum within which this investigation takes place. It's remarkable how much effort it takes to maintain a therapeutic stance with patients you love and hate. You've got a nice balance if you can fantasize about steamy sex in one hour and the use of a decapitating fire axe on a patient in the next hour. It keeps you on your toes.

You didn't know what you were getting into did you, Sigmund? However, you like doing what you're doing and hope you can survive your development into a psychiatrist. You know why they call it the "impossible profession."

So you do as much as you can to get a hold on this stuff — you read, talk with colleagues, meet with supervisors, get into your own therapy, and gain experience. Sometimes you feel as if the responsibility is overwhelming and you can't possibly do the job. You seek as many outlets as you can. If you're a musician, you might write songs, a poet could have a field day. You've tried those devices.

And now you've decided to sit down and share your struggle with the world.

You'll be able to rest for a while, thinking that you've gained something. If only that little voice didn't say you know that this is only an initial step on your journey. Say good-bye to your old coach for now. You'll inevitably meet again.

From 'LOVING PATIENTS' to 'FIRST WEEK IN JULY'

In response to the intensity of his loving emotions, Dr Andrew Brotman brought into play several of his personal resources. He made use of his sense of humor, he recalled his old baseball coach, and experienced a variety of internal conversations. Some of these conversations were between him and his supervisor, and some took place between two elements of his own personality. He could stand aside and observe his own intense inner experience and review some of the principles and concepts underlying his work as a psychotherapist.

He also reminded himself of the moral and ethical requirements of his position. Thoughts, feelings, and impulses are intrapsychic experiences. They need not be enacted nor even communicated to the patient. The clinician's restraint can protect the patient from possible harm. Autognostic examination of these experiences may result in benefit to the patient.

One of the valuable and rare qualities that these observations presented was the ability to view his experience as a part of his own development as a clinician. Reviewing an experience as a part of the progress in time and in personal development can be valuable in providing perspective and hope in a difficult emotional circumstance.

Dr Brotman distinguished between desires (intrapsychic) and actions (interpersonal). The result was a nonexploitive therapy for the patient. He was able to live up to his standards of ethics and to gain the satisfaction of having overcome a difficult challenge at a vulnerable time, the beginning of training.

The next essay shows us something about the impact of emergency situations on the resident during his first week of training. These are stressful in a different way.

Chapter 2

FIRST WEEK IN JULY

Arthur J. Barsky III, M.D.

He sweeps into the room ready to lecture the first person he can corral, my first manic patient. "I want to thank all of you for helping to develop the powers that I now have, for making me so unique. You know what a genius I am, and you've helped me to know it. I don't even know the limits of my ability yet. You people have put me through hell to prove myself, but now I can thank you for it. . . ." He takes off his jacket, loosens his tie, pacing like a Southern revivalist. The force of verbal and physical energy pushes me back into the chair, like a piece of paper blown into the corner when the door opens and the wind gusts in. Yet even with this ebullient, delusional businessman, there is an acknowledged sense of reason gone wrong. He doesn't need help. He is making perfect sense. He has never felt better in his life. Yet he agrees to swallow two tablespoons of red medicine. He feels frightened. "This is like a nightmare." But then, like the jolt of a ski lift when the slack snaps taut, he is off on the monologue again.

As the medication quells his inexhaustible energy and imagination, I arrange hospitalization. The boy's wealthy businessman father instantly engages top private psychiatric care near home. The capriciousness of the medical care process is evident. Had he been poor, separated from his family, a routine case, without good prognosis, he would have gone to the state hospital. Despite all the "science" of "modern medicine," the patient's treatment and psychiatric outcome are probably most influenced by such factors as wealth, health insurance, attractiveness, and intelligence.

I experience the cold fury of a serious suicide attempt. There are no histrionics, no awareness of an audience, no wish to stir others to help. Only the deadly, angry, cold intention. At 12:30 in the morning, entering the emergency room, the patient's daughter tells of returning early from a date to find mother sitting calmly at the kitchen table, windows closed, gas jets on. In Room Five the patient has her back to me and is on her knees. Her head is hyperextended by a taut white sheet ripped from the stretcher. It is knotted around her neck and tied over the intravenous pole inserted in the stretcher; the scene is so surrealistic that it takes me a second to appreciate what is really happening. As I unknot the sheet from around her neck she hardly struggles. There is only the tearful, furious stare, and eyes set in a stony and determined face. "I'm not crazy. I just want to be dead now." Now not even allowed the private act of taking her own life, she sits regally. She is dressed in the incongruous manner of patients swept up by relatives and brought to the emergency room. Old bermuda shorts, sleeveless blouse half-buttoned, slippers on grimy feet. There follows the indignity of her being placed in a room with no furniture, padded sound-proof walls, and a viewing window.

When I return she enacts the only bit of defiance left her. She stands firmly upright against the one wall in the room that cannot be seen through the viewing window. Only her feet show.

She is not wealthy, has no health insurance, and goes to the state hospital that serves her neighborhood.

Over the next 12 hours, the visceral anatomy of a mental breakdown is exposed. The progression from sanity to chaos. She is 32, teaches English and philosophy. She has a lovely, even suntan, short brown hair, neat blue and white sun dress, leather sandals. I notice her feet, because they are clean. I can't remember the last time I saw a patient with clean toenails. She is psychotic and a fragment of her observes and reports the whole process: "It's like my unconscious is cracking open and I'm able to look inside. . . . My subconscious is exploding." She feels staggering fear as she sees herself dissolved.

I, too, am afraid. At one point she begs, "I'm so afraid, help me." She is losing her grip and her sentences become more frantic: "You're God, and you're the only person on earth who can help me." She drifts off like a raft tearing free and floating downstream. And I on the bank have no line to pull per back. The urge to rescue is intense. But all my help, all my concern, 24 hours a day, 7 days a week, will not bridge the chasm that has opened here. I think of becoming a researcher and studying the pathogenesis of schizophrenia.

This girl both enthralls and disturbs me. I try to gain her trust, and I work hard to have her admitted to the well-staffed, well-run, teaching unit of our own hospital. Perhaps she is so poignant because she is attractive, because she is so intelligent and articulate, or just because of something so irrelevant as her being an English teacher.

I am called to see an agitated, drunken 15-year-old who has inflicted a minor laceration on his wrist. His face is sweaty and streaked with dirt, his T-shirt is torn. He is nasty and argumentative, yelling that the police are trying to railroad him into prison. The proof will emerge later this morning when he is scheduled to appear at the opening of his trial for auto theft! I leave him, secluded, with an attendant, to answer a phone call.

I next see him racing past nurses and security guards, out of the front door of the emergency ward. He has assaulted his attendant and fled. I see the small angular figure, silhouetted against the yellow light at the end of a dim hall. An hour later a trauma victim is rushed in, and the elaborate ballet of emergency care for the trauma victim begins. The ambulance attendants say the patient jumped from a downtown building.

It is the boy I was evaluating. He is now silent, bleeding. His arms are deformed by massive fractures, he is breathing in snorts, his abdominal wall swelling as blood accumulates beneath it.

The suddenness haunts me for weeks. The abusive teenager of one moment is the unconscious trauma victim the next. The healthy boy one moment lies mortally wounded the next. Where do such impulses come from? "Psychiatry is a lethal business," one of my supervisors says.

At the end of the week I am listening to a suicidal Vietnam veteran who begs not to be returned to the archaic, custodial hospital he has fled. He pleads for the opportunity to talk things out, to make peace with what he did in the war. He begs for help and it is hard not to respond — soon it is like trying to hospitalize a member of my own family. I spend four hours getting him admitted to a good community mental health center in violation of the rules that state he must return to a VA hospital. I argue with the VA administrators and doctors, cajole the authorities at the community mental health center, convince my supervisors to help me pull strings. After innumerable telephone conversations and four face-to-face conferences, I finally succeed. I go home exhausted and wonder if I can afford to get so emotionally invested in very many patients.

Learning psychiatry becomes intertwined with learning about myself, my limits. I learn to use my gut reactions. If I am delighted by a grandiose psychotic, he is probably manic — if I am frightened by him, he is probably schizophrenic. I learn how infantile a young woman is when, despite all her seductive talk, she turns me off. A 22-year-old former drug addict sobs by my desk as he describes returning to an empty apartment because his wife has run off with another man. As he cries, I wonder how many people have sat in that chair in as much pain in the 24 hours since I've been on duty. How many boxes of Kleenex have my patients gone through in the last week?

"When was the last time someone else was in your apartment?" He says, "Three months."

As a new psychiatrist I am learning how many people when asked "Who are the people in your life?" answer with "no one."

From 'FIRST WEEK IN JULY' to 'THE DEAD TEACH'

Dr Barsky reported what he observed and what he felt in the psychiatric emergency room. Learning psychiatry became intertwined with learning about his inner experience. The latter was not a substitute for the cognitive learning and educated thinking that must be performed by a physician. The emotions evoked by such experiences are hard to ignore. Avoidance of painful and shocked feelings, through suppression, denial, or other defenses, is possible. While protective, such mechanisms can be limiting and can lead to covert inner conflict. A clinician who is prepared can use such emotional experiences constructively, along with the cognitive processes more commonly associated with medical practice.

Chapter 3

THE DEAD TEACH

Joseph Deltito, M.D.

I remember the day I grew up as a doctor, a bitter winter's day three years ago. The chill hit me as I stepped out the back of my house that December morning, the coldest so far that winter. No doubt the next two months would be worse.

Driving a few blocks I saw that the local service station was being renovated. The heater in my car was not yet warmed up. Even my eyeballs were cold. They fixed on a young black man tearing up the sidewalk with a jackhammer. He did not wear a heavy arctic parka like mine, only a flimsy zip-up sweatshirt. Couldn't he afford a decent coat? Perhaps he had moved up North from Mississippi or Alabama, not realizing the severity of New England winters. Possibly the shakings of the jackhammer warmed him through accelerated metabolism. At any rate his face looked cold.

His task seemed terrible. I wondered how much he was paid to endure this torture, $5 or maybe $6 an hour? My thoughts turned to the cardiologists at the hospital. They would thread a long balloon-tipped tube down the jugular vein; the catheter would wedge into a blood vessel in a patient's lung. This tube allowed them to gather data about the patient's vital functions. The data from this tube would be displayed on an oscilloscope above the bed. How advanced, how fascinating, and, for the cardiologist, how lucrative. One hour's work might net $200.

Something seemed wrong. Shouldn't the man who had to suffer the jackhammer in the brutal New England winter be paid more than the cardiologist who has the intrinsic reward of saving lives using intelligence and modern technology? Would $6 an hour be enough to complement these rewards that the cardiologist reaped? The warmth finally started to dribble out of my Toyota's heater.

I was in the fifth month of my residency. So far I had learned enough to feel comfortable but not enough to be bored. The high point of my day was the therapy session with a 22-year-old woman weighing 84 lb. Anorexia nervosa. Every bony prominence of her body was a proud medal of her grand accomplishment in life, her ability to withstand the torture of starvation.

She had arrived on the Inpatient Unit two weeks after me. After months of intensive work, I seemed to be coming to an appreciation of my utter inability to understand her or the others who starved themselves. During the past months I had become more and more preoccupied with this patient. After she left my office that afternoon, as I stood up from my desk, I noticed my pants were looser. I pulled in my belt another notch. Was it coincidence that I had lost 30 lb during the past months? Could my preoccupation with this patient have led me to persevere on my eternal diet? Before, it never lasted for more than a week.

I let my emotions run. I felt challenged by her. An imaginery glove slapped across my face. An appointment at dawn? Sabers? Pistols? No, these were not the chosen weapons, but salads instead of lasagna and stairs instead of elevators. She would do anything to avoid, or burn off, calories. The fact that I had lost so much weight suggested the tremendous influence the patient wielded. She was no longer the frail little girl of summer, but the formidable enemy of winter. Her anorexia was her strength, tyranny over her family, and control over all others. My pity solidified into respect. Now I was able to respond to her caustic manipulations with strength matched to the task.

I was rushing through my afternoon's notes. It was my turn to take calls at the state hospital. I arrived a bit late, just after 6 PM.

Four admissions were waiting for me. Each workup entailed a history, performing a physical examination, and ordering medications. The nurse said that three of the four patients were restrained and the fourth was having a cigarette with her boyfriend. The only unfettered patient was a middle-aged woman calmly smoking a cigarette and sitting across from her middle-aged boyfriend. A smile would fleetingly light up her weather-beaten face. I decided to work her up last. After five harried hours I completed the notes on the last of my three agitated, psychotic patients. All had responded to injections of an antipsychotic drug. Their restraints were now off.

It was now 11:30 — one more patient to go. Her papers read "schizophrenic in decompensation. Patient demonstrating bizarre behavior."

Her boyfriend described behavior that was indeed bizarre. Over the months she was almost continuously chain-smoking, definitely a change. She frequently had bowel movements in her pants and made no effort to clean herself. She was giddy and seemed to lack a certain general social appropriateness that had been there before. Yes, she carried a psychiatric diagnosis and had decompensated many times before. But she always became fearful that someone was trying to hurt her, and she would hear voices taunting her to kill herself. Something was different in her current state.

After taking a brief history I went on to the physical examination. The first abnormality was the gross inequality of the size of her pupils. Her left pupil was larger than her right. Shining a penlight in her eyes failed to elicit the characteristic contraction of her pupil. When the bottoms of her feet were stroked with a sharp key, a standard test, her left big toe curled under a bit, her right large toe extended upwards — a subtle finding, but one that started my heart beating more quickly. I took her blood pressure. It was so high that I almost thought the mercury would squirt out of its glass. She told me she had problems with hypertension in the past several months.

High blood pressure, nonreactive dilated pupil, upgoing toe, socially inappropriate behavior — all suggested the frontal portion of this woman's brain had been compromised by some intracranial catastrophe, probably the result of several leaks into the frontal lobe from blood vessels ruptured by high pressure. I called the emergency room of my own hospital. While petitioning the neurologist to accept the transfer of this patient to his care, I was met with a bombardment of neurophysiological explanations of how this patient could have all the signs and symptoms of a stroke and not be seriously ill. Yet I knew she was ill! I wondered if he did also.

Because transfer for this patient was refused, I medicated her to lower the blood pressure. I told the nurse to check her pressure every hour throughout the night and to call me if it went over 160/110. I then lay down to a very tentative sleep. A half hour later the door rattled from a furious knocking. "Doctor, come quick, the patient is seizing." Expecting to see a flailing convulsive fit, I was, for a split second, relieved to see her lying calmly. But she was too calm. Not even her lungs were moving. She had no pulse.

I yelled to the nurse to get the code cart and defibrillator. She ran from the room. Two mental health workers seemed paralyzed. The one other person in the room was a chronic schizophrenic named John who seemed more attuned and appropriate to this situation than I had ever seen him before. "What do we do, Doctor?" I showed him how to compress her chest while I was to perform mouth-to-mouth breathing. As I lowered my mouth to blow air into her lungs, I saw it was full of vomit. I reached my fingers in and scooped out as much as I could.

I hesitated for a few seconds. How can you do this, I thought. How can you blow into that mouth of vomit? I argued with myself hoping to find a way to perform the disgusting task. The notion flickered that this was the charitable thing to do, the Christian act. I moved my head closer to her mouth, but a gap remained. Stronger argument was needed to bring our lips together.

In the background of my mind hung the young black man working the jackhammer in the frigid cold. Society didn't expect him to perform the revolting task before me, it expected me to do it. I got closer, but I still couldn't do it.

I pictured a fireman about to run into a burning building to rescue a child.

Suddenly I made myself bend down. My stomach churned. I turned my face aside and vomited a little myself, and quickly returned to the task.

The nurse finally arrived with the endotracheal tube, which I pushed past her putrid vocal cords into the trachea. A large black vinyl bag was connected to this tube, and by the squeezing of a hand its bellows pumped air into her.

A large-bore catheter threaded into the jugular vein in her neck let me give the medication her heart needed. I remembered assisting a cardiologist last year in a similar procedure. His services commanded $200 an hour at that time, but what price could be placed on his instruction in the technique I was now using?

The patient's heart began to beat again, her lungs began to move on their own. Her white and clammy faced turned pink and warm.

The ambulance arrived to take her to the general hospital. She never regained consciousness and died at dawn. The autopsy revealed a recent bleed from a ruptured blood vessel in her brain. There was evidence of several old bleeds, particularly in the frontal lobes.

In my personal postmortem, I realized my free-flowing experiences of emotion were all barometers that were sensitive to the pressures of those around me. From the anorectic patient I could see how vulnerable I was to a personal challenge, how dieting could now be motivated, that what really motivates me is that sense of personal challenge. At the point when I needed supreme motivation to perform, I could conjure up imagery that turned the resuscitation into a reflection of my own self.

From 'THE DEAD TEACH' to 'THE WEIGHT'

Dr Deltito told us how he learned that he is vulnerable to personal challenge. At the same time he showed us that his response to personal challenge was one of his strengths in a situation that would be repugnant to most people and was revolting to him. He was able to drive himself ahead using free associations.

Like many well-trained and competent physicians, Dr Deltito is a sharp observer. In addition, he is cognizant of his observations and he reflects on them. He observes the internal perceptions and ideas that come to his mind spontaneously. In addition, he has the ability to direct his images, as in bringing up the picture of the fireman entering the building.

The following vignette provides us with a personal involvement of another kind.

Chapter 4

THE WEIGHT

R. Bruce Lydiard, Ph.D., M.D.

The transition from medical internship to first-year psychiatry was one I'd looked forward to. I thought I was well-suited to psychiatry. Despite the occasional pain it caused, I valued caring and personal involvement with my medical patients. My first assignment in psychiatry was in the Acute Psychiatric Service. I was a bit put off by the indifference of the senior residents toward some of the patients we interviewed together during the first week or so. Not me, I thought. I'm going to keep my heart open wide.

Early one evening while I was on call, a young woman came to me with two small children in tow. After we sat down in the interviewing room, tears welled in her eyes as she related how she'd been abandoned by her boyfriend with whom she and her children had been living in a motel room. Her husband had left her months earlier, and she had to go on welfare and moved in with her mother. After she met her boyfriend, her mother threw her out. The boyfriend decided abruptly to leave her, and she had come for help finding shelter. She asked me to find a place where the children would be safe.

I got busy calling around. The secretary interrupted a few minutes later and asked that the young woman take her rambunctious children to the main lobby to avoid setting off some of the edgier psychotic patients waiting to be seen. The woman asked me if she could borrow a cigarette and a dime for a phone call, which

I gladly provided. I continued to call, very concerned that I find proper lodging for this family. After several calls, I found a shelter that might be suitable. I went down to find her and saw her sitting in a phone booth, chattering and laughing as her children raced about the main lobby. As I got closer, I noticed she had a full pack of cigarettes and over a dollar in change on the phone stand. The shelter, she said, was too far away and wouldn't do.

At that moment I learned my first real lesson of survival in psychiatry: I had become responsible for her. As she sat chattering on the phone, I was sweating. She was calm; I felt awful. I had allowed the weight of her problems to be slipped onto my shoulders and hadn't even realized it. But I certainly had felt it.

I suggested that she ought to play a more central role in controlling her destiny. I handed her the list of shelters, led her and her children back up the hall into an empty interviewing room with a phone, and went to see another patient. The secretary later told me she had left after about 15 minutes to stay with a friend.

This early experience was one of the most important in my training. I learned how important it is to define whose problem it was that I was dealing with. My problem was the need to be a successful caregiver and not to disappoint anyone. I had been doing this young woman's worrying for her — feeling her anxiety, so to speak — rather than helping her learn how to carry her own burdens.

From 'THE WEIGHT' to 'SHADOW BOXING'

Tender-hearted, young clinicians are often easy marks for manipulative patients. Sometimes a series of experiences such as the one described in "The Weight" can build to a crescendo of disillusionment. They may gradually lead to hardness and indifference. Dr Lydiard was able to recognize what had been going on: both the patient's manipulations and his own susceptibility.

Instead of disillusionment, he learned that setting limits is one of the ways that he might be helpful to this patient and to others like her but not lose tenderness and humane interest.

In the following essay, Dr Gary Sachs discusses a patient who inflicted great pain upon herself. Dr Sachs suffered along with the patient in some complicated ways as he describes to us in "Shadow Boxing."

Chapter 5

SHADOW BOXING

Gary Sachs, M.D.

I watch Ms Z bang her head on the floor, and it reminds me of the point in a dream when something so significant happens that consciousness intrudes to say it's just a dream. As I watch Ms Z scream and thrash, the dreamy sensation comes over me several times, but the experience remains real. After a few minutes she gets up, excuses her "childishness," and proceeds with the session — as if the episode made not the slightest impact on her or me.

And like the 100 self-abusive physical tantrums I witnessed during the 15 months in therapy with this 25-year-old anorexic, I again respond as if nothing unusual had happened. I write a progress note aware that I feel uncomfortable but unsure why. After all, colleagues concerned for my safety interrupted 18 past sessions, and this session created so little disruption that nobody even commented on it when I walked out. So I leave reassuring myself that everything is okay.

During the next few days I find myself repeatedly presenting the case to my fellow residents, other supervisors, and even my wife. They know as well as I that it isn't advice I need. Limits need to be set, everyone agrees, but why didn't I do it already? Am I angry at the patient, sadistically enjoying her suffering?

During the first four months of treatment, the patient and other caregivers told me about Ms Z's tantrums. The first time she actually hit herself during a therapy session, I asked her to stop and she did. Later she said my intervention indicated to her that I cared only about myself, "just like my family who don't want to know about my suffering." Furthermore, in my supervisor's opinion, I made "a cloud out of a silver lining" by not recognizing that Ms Z was showing me how she was outside the therapy room. At the time believing this, when the hitting resumed, I tried to be more empathic. Little progress occurred as I tried in many ways to understand and interpret the behavior. In supervision I described the discomfort I felt observing the patient shriek and hit herself (over 100 times some sessions. . . I counted), but I never again prohibited the behavior. The work seemed futile; the year ended; my supervisor's written evaluation included the observation that I had "difficulty tolerating the patient's sadness."

I hoped the next supervisor would tell me I "must" terminate the impossible case. I admitted this to the new supervisor and told him how unhappy I felt about receiving a negative evaluation of my work. Things improved in the therapy. But after a few fresh interpretations of the self-abuse fell flat, the supervisor intervened, suggesting I simply show no reaction at all. Some progress followed despite frequent episodes of Ms Z delivering forceful punches to her own face, abdomen, and pelvis. This progress seemed to justify continuing the strategy, and in a few months I found myself disagreeing with the supervisor, who now said I should set limits and prohibit the hitting behavior.

Nanometers could measure the progress that justified my continued nonresponse to her violence. Why then did I continue to tolerate such untherapeutic behavior? Simplistically, I thought I should because the first supervisor said so. Though true to some extent, it hides more than it illuminates. I suffered a double wound by virtue of the lack of progress and the first supervisor's negative evaluation, but some comforts were now in hand. Because the patient created a loud disturbance, most of the clinic staff—not only my supervisor—knew I sat with a "very difficult case." Proving myself able to tolerate this removed the tarnish from my self-esteem. Stopping her from hitting herself might prove the first supervisor correct—showing me to be an inferior therapist.

The second supervisor suggested that the patient's hitting represented a way of gaining by a negative behavior and so maintained her low self-esteem. Mimicking this, my discomfort in watching her was as self-inflicted as her actual self-flagellation. I too benefitted in a way that ultimately lowered my self-esteem. Her distorted body image was paralleled by my distortion of myself as a beginning therapist — both of us striving for a caricature of perfection. My pride had kept me figuratively banging my head against the wall in tolerating her behavior.

After admitting error in tolerating her self-abuse, I tell her any meeting in which she hits herself will be ended immediately. She accepts this, hitting herself only three times in the next ten sessions. When we resume meeting after the third truncated session, she announces she finds the arrangement intolerable — she wants to continue her treatment at a local community clinic. We agree to terminate after five additional meetings. Over this period, though she again experiences many of the same feelings that used to trigger tantrums, she never hits herself. Making this observation at the last meeting she wonders whether she really needs to terminate, but she fears this sentiment is an artifact of the termination. We agree to meet in six weeks for consultation so she can reconsider her options.

From 'SHADOW BOXING' to 'NIGHT PEOPLE'

Dr Sachs' main discovery about himself in this psychotherapeutic experience was that his pride could obscure his better judgment. The threat to his pride, however, was only one of three major sources of stress to which he was subjected. The second source was the patient's bizarre behavior. The third is the inherent complexity of psychotherapeutic problems with the resultant disagreement and sometimes confusion among practitioners and even among supervisors.

Dr Sachs' first supervisor thought that the head banging should be permitted to continue because it represented an honest disclosure to the therapist of the patient's behavior outside the treatment situation. Evidently, that supervisor thought that if the head-banging were discouraged, the patient would infer that the psychotherapist did not really want to know or to observe how the patient behaved outside. The second supervisor had other ideas.

My own view is that action, especially violent action, has no place in the psychotherapeutic situation. Psychotherapy is primarily a verbal form of treatment. It was known from the beginning as the "talking therapy." In psychotherapy, ideas, attitudes, and feelings need to be expressed vocally as much as possible. Naturally, much expression takes place in nonverbal forms such as tone of voice, facial expression, physical posture, and paraverbal forms such as choice of words and accent.

Physical action going beyond such expressions has a tendency to discharge impulses, ideas, emotions, and fantasies in such a way as to lose them from the therapeutic interaction. Violent action, of course, can produce harmful and sometimes irreversible effects.

One of the general objectives of psychotherapy is the integration of cognitive with emotional experiences in the patient. If emotional experiences, such as self-directed rage, are expressed grossly in a nonverbal way, such integration is made more difficult.

The principle of confining psychotherapeutic interactions to verbal and paraverbal expressions is widely supported. Many opportunities for disagreement arise, even among those who favor verbalization. At what point does an acceptable, useful, and expressive nonverbal gesture become an undesirable and counterproductive action? Differences of judgment about such quantitative variations can be complicated. Of course, in the instance that Dr Sachs reported, the action was clearly violent.

Differences of opinion and judgment occur even in the most scientific aspects of medicine. We have disputes about the value of coronary artery bypass grafts as opposed to conservative medical treatment of coronary artery disease. In the area of prevention of cancer of the gastrointestinal tract, considerable controversy centers around the value of fiber in the diet. In the biological aspects of psychiatry, the usefulness and safety of electroconvulsive therapy are avidly debated.

In the area of psychotherapy, clear objective data are even less available than in these other more objective fields. The uncertainties are stressful on practitioners in general. Young physicians in training experience intensified stress when the conflicting opinions of teachers are presented in pejorative terms. In my opinion, the original attack on Dr Sachs' pride was unwarranted. Once it had occurred, however, it became a burden in this treatment situation. To his credit and to his ultimate benefit, Dr Sachs was able eventually to discover the subtle maneuvering that his pride took in the situation.

The next essay, "Night People," illustrates the emotional pounding that patients may inflict on psychiatrists. Direct accusations designed to arouse guilt and remorse were added to the frustration, disappointment, and tattered compassion experienced by Dr Mark Pollack. But it was not this recriminating hostility that aroused his autognostic effort. It was a deeper connection.

Chapter 6

NIGHT PEOPLE

Mark Harris Pollack, M.D.

Mr Jonas was found dead on the floor of his room. Half-empty bottles of antidepressants and liquor were strewn around his body. His death in a boarding house had the same pathetic ineffectuality his life had. In the end, nobody was quite sure whether he intended to die, or had bungled yet another in a long series of suicidal gestures. I didn't hear about it until weeks afterward, and beyond commenting on its inevitability in a strained voice, I remained outwardly unmoved.

Mr Jonas was my very first patient. I had started residency at the state hospital the day I met him. He was lying face down on a cot in the seclusion room wearing dark sunglasses, and pieces of wax were stuck in his ears. They had him in seclusion for eloping and for attempting to hang himself by tying a shoelace around his neck and holding it over his head as he jumped off four or five stairs. When the mental health worker told me the story, I laughed. But it was the same embarrassed laughter you hear at a prize fight watching a clumsy boxer beaten about the ring by a superior opponent.

He accepted the invitation to come to my office, answering my questions in terse, flat tones. When I offered him coffee, he reacted with surprise and took off his sunglasses and removed the earplugs. He became animated with a shy eagerness as he related his life story. His mother had died in a mental hospital when he was

6 years old. He remembered with shame hiding behind a tree when she came home on pass so the neighbors wouldn't know he was her child.

At age 12, he would sexually service his older brother, a relationship he found somehow comforting, but it ended when his brother found a girlfriend. At age 14 he became the sole caretaker of an alcoholic, abusive, invalid father, whose death when the patient was 28 led to the first of many suicide attempts and hospitalizations. He drank heavily for years, saw innumerable therapists, had no friends, no lovers, no relationships, no steady jobs. The high point of his life came when he was interviewed for a case conference by the famous Dr Elvin Semrad at the Massachusetts Mental Health Center — although he was long since unable to remember anything about the conference except being on stage before a large auditorium full of people.

As the first weeks of this treatment went by, his anger and isolation were seemingly diminished and were replaced by expressions of sadness and longing for a sense of being cared for, a feeling he said he never experienced. The symptoms of his depression responded to antidepressants and lithium. In almost daily sessions he remembered his past and planned for the future. His rapid progress was encouraging, and I was proud of his improvement. I was somewhat surprised by the pessimism expressed by the more experienced residents whom I assumed were deficient in the empathy and compassion that I possessed in abundance. Mr Jonas' depression lifted as he expressed his anger at the people who all his life exploited and abandoned him.

Two months into the hospitalization as we began to plan for discharge, Mr Jonas' behavior changed. He sabotaged a number of housing and job placements that were arranged for him. He would take a pass to look for housing and work and come back days later drunk and screeching threats at the nurses.

I was bewildered and angered. My supervisors were not surprised that his recovery crumbled as the day of discharge approached. I read more about borderline personalities, interpreted his feelings of rage at my abandonment of him, and confronted the split that he had created between the nursing staff and me. I adjusted his medication and set up his outpatient day treatment program.

The drinking and acting out continued. I wanted to treat Mr Jonas as an outpatient, but overwhelmed by the thought of midnight phone calls, suicide attempts, and hospitalizations, I was secretly relieved when my supervisor talked about "rescue fantasies" and suggested that the nature and intensity of his relationship with caregivers argued for a more diffused system of care — group, day treatment, and medication clinic.

On the day of discharge, Mr Jonas came to my office and said, "Thank you for taking such good care of me." After grinding his cigarette butt out on the floor of my office, he left for a shelter for the homeless after rejecting our last boarding house placement. It was a relief to have respite from his sarcasm and hatefulness, but I felt a peculiar mix of sadness and disappointment and guilt. And I was angry at him for destroying my "cure."

I listened for news of Mr Jonas for many months. It seemed that he had made a good connection with the outpatient clinic. At first, he had not gone at all and then would show up drunk, but he finally settled down and came regularly for a while. We didn't find out until after his death about his attempts to get therapists at a number of different clinics in the Boston area by altering his history and denying his current involvement with our system.

His boarding house, like my apartment, was near the hospital, and Mr Jonas would occasionally appear at my side as I stood waiting for the stoplight to change on my way to work. I felt enraged and guilty during these ambushes outside the sanctuary of my office. He'd say, "Doctor — did you hear, I took an overdose last night. It was the lithium you gave me. I'm drinking again. I'm stuck in that lousy room. . . no job." The light would change and I would tell him without much enthusiasm that if he wanted to talk to me about it, we could set up a time in my office, but he never did.

After I rotated off the state hospital, I worked six months in the emergency room. I lost track of Mr Jonas until one night toward the end of my rotation, the transit police brought him in drunk, kicking, spitting, and swearing. He had jumped onto the subway tracks directly in front of two officers, who had easily pulled him back onto the platform. As the security guards carried him by in restraints, he started screaming, "Doctor! Doctor! You discharged me too soon."

I went to the back ward. He was lying there mute, staring up at the ceiling, and when I took off his glasses his eyes were black and cold. Despite my fatigue in the late hour and the imperturbability I had developed through the many nights in the emergency room, the eyes frightened me. I sent him to the state hospital that night and never saw him again.

After his death, I went back to check the emergency room files. Mr Jonas was discharged from the hospital the day after his admission there, a not infrequent experience for the chronic patients who present to crowded state facilities after midnight suicide gestures and are judged in the morning to be in no imminent danger. I was relieved to discover that he had been in the emergency room a number of times after our last encounter — I hadn't "touched him last," no one could fault me. But I never asked whether the pill bottles by his body were ones I gave him.

When I think back, it is with affection and sadness. Even if I hadn't promised Mr Jonas more than I could deliver and then had been disappointed in myself and angered with him when he called me on it, I don't think it would have turned out much differently. Mr. Jonas left many people unmoved and others perhaps too moved to accept what he made the responsibility for keeping him alive. The thought that my rejection was the one that caused him to kill himself is both absurd and frightening. I don't even know whether he wanted his life to end that night.

Mr Jonas reminds me of a night I spent camping on an island off the coast of Maine. I awoke alone in the middle of the night, the only light was the moon. My tarp on an exposed ledge overlooked a small cove. Alone in the darkness, I panicked and ran down to the beach. Left behind by the receding tide I screamed, and I filled the night with my sounds and contained my death fear by the shock of cold air on my naked body.

After some time, I returned exhausted to my sleeping bag. The pain from my feet, bloodied by the sharp stones, reassured me of reality, and my movements and echoes populated the black with at least some presence.

Mr Jonas spent most of his life in that black and was unable to find anything in it of comfort, of reassurance. The ambiguity of his death fit: He dissolved into night, like vapors off a block of ice, leaving behind nothing to mark his existence, except perhaps the questions in my mind.

I wonder, had I become his therapist, would he be alive today? Or would my relationship with him prove an illusion vaporizing in the daylight? He lived isolated, alone, without any source of nurturance or soothing and no presence inside to anchor him when he was in danger of drifting off into the night.

From 'NIGHT PEOPLE' to 'A MUZZLE FOR YOUR SHEEP'

Dr Pollack hadn't "touched Mr Jonas last," but it is evident that Mr Jonas had touched Dr Pollack lastingly.

Despite his understanding of the situation, Dr Pollack still felt a great sense of responsibility, perhaps even a sense of guilt in relation to the patient's suffering and eventual death. He was able to recognize his emotional kinship with Mr Jonas through his memory of the frightening experience of being alone on an island. The desperate need for contact was somewhat similar, at least for that moment in the doctor's life. The two men differed enormously, though, in terms of their abilities to derive comfort and satisfaction from contact with other people. Their capacities for adapting to life differed immensely. Underneath, however, there was a human similarity that linked the doctor and the patient.

Dr Pollack mentioned relatively quick discharge of patients from the state hospital. I wonder about Mr Jonas' response had he been given a long-term hospital experience. Mr Jonas had received several courses of outpatient psychotherapy, and all of them had been unsuccessful. It seems improbable that outpatient psychotherapy, even with the caring responsiveness of Dr Pollack, would have had a much different outcome. Meanwhile, we read that Mr Jonas responded very positively to his inpatient experience. Difficulties arose only when plans were made for his discharge.

In the current thrust toward deinstitutionalization, long-term hospitalization is rarely available. Possibly Mr Jonas may have been another victim of deinstitutionalization. He is clearly someone who was unable to adjust his life outside the hospital despite the efforts of many agencies and mental health professionals. He was the beneficiary of modern psychopharmacologic treatment and seems to have been given a variety of psychosocial treatments, all of which failed. The information available to us in "Night People" strongly suggests that a long period of inpatient treatment may have led to Mr Jonas' improvement. It is possible that it may have prolonged his survival.

The institutional limitations imposed on the state hospital in terms of funding, bed space, and facilities make the provision of long-term hospitalization extremely difficult. It is a form of treatment that is seldom permitted.

There is no way of proving that long-term treatment would have made much of a difference. It is my inference as a clinician. Dr Pollack hinted at this possibility though he did not emphasize it. Professionals like Dr Pollack are expected to accomplish what is often impossible. They are required to provide treatment and protection for severely impaired patients without adequate facilities. This imposes considerable stress. Lacking opportunities for prolonged inpatient treatment for these patients, physicians and other mental health professionals must provide care with whatever they have available. One of the consequences is the tormenting sense of doubt, even guilt, that may remain with the conscientious caregivers. For the patients, the effects may be suffering, homelessness, and death.

Another example of a tenuous contact between a deeply troubled patient and an empathic physician is presented in "A Muzzle for Your Sheep."

Chapter 7

A MUZZLE FOR YOUR SHEEP

*A Resident**

The night had fallen. I had let my tools drop from my hands. Of what moment now was my hammer, my bolt, or thirst, or death? On one star, one planet, my planet, the Earth, there was a little prince to be comforted. I took him in my arms, and rocked him. I said to him: "The flower that you love is not in danger. I will draw you a muzzle for your sheep. I will draw you a railing to put around your flower. I will — "

I did not know what to say to him. I felt awkward and blundering. I did not know how I could reach him, where I could overtake him and go on hand in hand with him once more.

It is such a secret place, the land of tears.

(From *The Little Prince*, Antoine de Saint-Exupéry)

The land of tears is crossed and recrossed in the course of a psychiatrist's day, during each journey, 50 minutes at a time. Images roam through my mind, lost creatures searching for their appropriate master, an association, a past experience that helps make sense of the present, images once not so free-flowing or easily connected until, in the process of my own analysis, my unconscious was awakened from its deep slumber. There I found my share of

---

Editor's Note: The author of "A Muzzle for Your Sheep" asked not to be identified by name, because such identification might have adversely affected other therapeutic work.

33

wandering beasts — some gentle, some sad, some violent and un-assuaged. The process of owning and taming them has been painful, often rendering the therapeutic boundary paper-thin.

The other day a psychotic patient looked at me in the throes of his paranoid fear and said, "I am so alone and disconnected. The world is a hostile and scary place. There is no warmth." My mind called up an image of him as a child, cowering, and I couldn't conjure up his parents. Where were they?...then?...now? Present, but not felt? I'll never know, but here's an opportunity for warmth. What can I say that won't frighten him further? How does one connect when warmth may be felt as smothering, when caring may be felt as controlling?

Looking at him directly I asked, "Do you trust me?"

"I'm trying to, Doctor."

The link was fragile, susceptible to a break at any point. My mind was a void, I was feeling his emptiness, and it temporarily paralyzed me. I said, "But you're here speaking to me — that must have taken a lot of courage." A flicker of a smile appeared at the corners of his mouth, his frightened features softened, his eyes filled with tears. I felt my own well up. The link was growing stronger. From the void, he was allowing himself to be reeled in, to be among warm bodies again.

"Despite your feelings, you're taking the risk of connecting..."

"I trust you, Doctor, even if the world is cold..."

The encounter ends, he returns to the ward, wandering among the broken spirits and twisted bodies of the chronically psychotic. I ask myself, how long can that flicker of warmth last? Will it maintain him when he gets pushed in the lunch line, robbed by another patient, or avoided by passers-by on the street?

The next week, anticipating discharge, the patient progressively withdrew back into the void, becoming increasingly uncommunicative. Relatives failed to come forward to help. I went to see him in the locked unit, where he had been transferred. Huddled in the corner, he did not respond to his name and averted his eyes. The image of a wounded animal came to mind. Now there was fear and hurt to overcome. I sat quietly near him, wondering again how to reel him back.

"You know, you're not alone..."

He stayed huddled and rigid, then barked, "Get away!" One doesn't freely approach wounded animals, yet one doesn't leave them to die. His dark emptiness returned to my mind.

"Whenever you're ready to talk."

"Get away." The flicker of warmth was gone. Only the fear was palpable. Distance was the only way for now.

Three days later, he came to my office. "I think I'm ready to try the outside again...you're leaving here soon also, aren't you? They all change. Nothing ever lasts."

We shook hands. The flicker was there as our eyes met. But I asked God, who will fan it next and help him keep it alive?

From 'A MUZZLE FOR YOUR SHEEP' to 'DESCENT INTO EGYPT'

The image of the patient as a child cowering and alone is an example of free association. The author imagined the absence of parents, which extended comprehension of the patient's plight. He was fearful of contact and yet needed contact to go on. The doctor applied this insight to the delicate interaction with the patient.

The slender connection, which was soon to be severed by the reality of the treatment situation, seems to have been constructive. It was a potential building block in a therapeutic structure.

The prospect of separation from the hospital disturbed this patient as it had Mr Jonas, described in the previous essay.

Free association is connected with the development of psychoanalysis and discoveries by Sigmund Freud. Awareness of freely floating and spontaneous imagery is actually a natural part of human mental functioning. Often it goes unnoticed because it seems to be disordered, illogical, and not obviously relevant to the circumstances of the moment. From their early years, children are trained to be logical and orderly in their thinking and in their speech. Freud referred to this rational form of thinking as secondary process. He referred to spontaneous imagery as part of primary process. This term described the workings of the dynamic unconscious. The therapeutic and investigative method known as psychoanalysis attempts to focus attention on the products of primary process, to provide a fuller understanding of the analysand's inner self.

Some people spontaneously develop their inner perceptiveness to recognize the importance and usefulness that can be derived from primary process experience. Others can learn this skill. The author of "A Muzzle for Your Sheep" performed the work described prior to any psychoanalytic experience. Similarly, the author of "Descent into Egypt" utilized his own dreams to enhance and deepen his understanding of his personal experience.

Looking back at the course of his life on the way to becoming a psychiatrist, Dr Paul Summergrad describes the pivotal function of two of his dreams. This essay also shows how dreams synthesize understanding even apart from the psychoanalytic process.

Chapter 8

DESCENT INTO EGYPT,
Genesis 37:36

Paul Summergrad, M.D.

He reduced Himself, as it were, down to the lowest of rungs, until a part of God above was placed into the darkness of matter. The intent of this was that the lower rungs themselves be uplifted so that there be "A greater light that comes from darkness." [Ecclesiastes 2:13]. This was the meaning of Joseph's descent into Egypt, the lowest of rungs, the narrow strait in the Great Sea. Through him joy was to be increased and the light brightened, for joy is greater when it has been lifted out of darkness.

Rabbi Menahem Nahum of Chernobyl (1730–1797)
Translated by A. Green

It was inevitable, I suppose, that it began with failure, echoing as it did much earlier losses. I was 17, a senior in high school in the spring of 1967. My hair was just edging over my collar.

I grew up in a loving, but overprotective, leftist Jewish secular home, first in the Bronx, then in Westchester County. I was immersed early in the world of a New York Jewish Ghetto, and it permeated me more than I knew. Till that spring I had never known true failure. I had always done well in school, aiming for a moderately intellectual college experience. I wanted to go off to college and study the history of human culture, philosophy, politics, to learn what was really known about human nature and eventually become a psychiatrist. An enormous amount of my self-esteem was invested in being verbal, bright, and intellectual.

In the spring of 1967, most of that began to fall apart. It seems trivial now. I wasn't accepted by any of the universities that I wanted and was forced to go to the State University of New York at Buffalo. I didn't understand why it happened. It made no sense. I experienced it as an enormous blow. When the fall came, I left for Buffalo and immediately became alienated. Buffalo was a pit of enormous proportions. I was hurt, enraged, isolated. What I saw was the petty ugliness of Main Street (the main street in Buffalo), the horror of the escalating war in Vietnam, and the seeming venality of America. I experienced a sense of total isolation from all familiar points of view — Marxism, Freudism, religion, politics as usual, Jewish humanism — all seemed utterly inadequate as explanatory systems. Life seemed filled with a degree of pain and suffering for which there could never be any adequate remedy. I plunged into the counterculture of the late sixties and, with the exception of a few Bob Dylan records and two close friends, nothing and no one spoke my language.

In the spring of 1968 after protestors imprisoned one Dow Chemical recruiter in the campus library and marched on the Pentagon, the world changed in that temporary intense way which Abraham Maslow termed a peak experience. It was early evening. On a brisk spring night I walked near a dingy overpass on Main Street with my friend Ira. I remember saying to him, "I'm having a profoundly religious experience."

During this experience, my view of the nature of reality was shattered. I looked about and realized that time as I had usually experienced it was ended. I was, the world was, everything was in Eternity, always had been, always would be. In truth, it was obvious that no delineated form had anything other than provisional reality, and in ultimate terms, all of reality was uncreated. Things would change shape and form but in their essence had no beginning or end. Indeed, where I was standing — where we all stand — is the Void, is Heaven, is Nirvana itself. Insight upon insight poured in, in a cascade. I was whole and complete exactly as I was. There was nothing to strive after in order to complete myself. I, and all living beings, were intrinsically complete, and always had been. I was overcome with awe. I had entered a state of multiple paradoxes. I was as dust with the deepest sense of humility before the perfection of the Universe. I owned nothing, I was in a state of complete poverty of the spirit. It seemed clear why priests took vows of poverty: there was nothing that one could truly possess, everything was possessed by God. Yet at the same time I was the richest man in the universe. There was not an iota of the world, even this hated street, which was not totally filled by the presence of God. When seen under the aspect of Eternity, all things were in perfect order. The universe was filled with mercy with unending compassion and grace, and all things moved forever deeper into the experience and fullness of God. I stood in the Tao, in the Midst of the Ein Sof. This was the beginning and the end, the source, aim, and the substance of all being. Nothing could ever be greater or more perfect than this, moving eternally into greater and greater degrees of perfection, of Tsuvah, of return.

It was a bit hard to go back to school after such an experience. What could mere words or books be now? The question was how to get back to this state as fully as possible.

In the summer of 1970, after a fairly circuitous route, I ended up at the Zen Center in Rochester, which was run by an American who had spent 13 years training in Japan under two of the most highly respected modern masters. I began the practice of Zen, aiming I thought for the experience of awakening — of enlightenment. For the first year I was there I did Zazen (Zen meditation) five to six hours a day while working on various construction projects at the center. The discipline and the training were arduous but extraordinarily beneficial. I learned more about intense self-discipline than I had in my previous 21 years. After a year, I continued my Zen meditation at an equal pace, attended a number of four-day meditation retreats where we sat 12 hours a day in an intense push to enlightenment. I started working as a substitute teacher and decided to live alone. I was now 22 and began to feel that I had to make some decisions. If I wasn't going to be a Zen Buddhist monk, which I wasn't, then I had to find some form of work within the dominant culture. I had always felt that in some sense I was still pursuing my old goal of becoming a psychiatrist. Yet I could find no way to fuse my religious experiences with psychodynamic psychiatry or Judaism. I was stuck—multiple streams of Western and Eastern thought and experience fought one another inside myself. I felt more strongly than ever the deep need to be alone. I saw some friends, but I cut myself off from all extraneous input, movies, books, TV, radio, newspapers, magazines. The sense of crisis intensified. I had no idea of how I could possibly go on.

After 8 months, I realized how much my youthful rage had been a product not of my social conscience but of anger at not getting what I wanted when I was 18. I was furious at being hurt, but for the first time could turn around and see that my struggle for enlightenment, while ultimately valid, was an attempt to transcend my real needs for the world. At this time I had the first of two important dreams.

In the first dream, I was in a field, following my Zen teacher and others walking up a high mountain. On the way I dropped my watch. I said to myself that I didn't really need the watch anyway, I would get beyond it and continued climbing. After a few more moments it became obvious that I absolutely had to go back to get the watch, and climbed down.

The dream seemed immediately clear to me. The watch was my need for the world of space and limits. I could no longer transcend them by climbing to enlightenment.

But the more fundamental problem remained unsolved—how to be Jewish, psychiatric, libidinal in the world, and yet religious and open. No resolution to that problem had occurred. I only knew what would no longer work.

A few weeks later I had a Great Dream.

In the dream, I am sitting talking with an Israeli friend of mine named Yossi. He is sitting across from me at a table and is suddenly surrounded by a dozen Arabs. The situation becomes very tense. The scene shifts and I am standing on a mountain overlooking a lake. Yossi is at the near shore with the 12 Arabs surrounding him in a semicircle. They are about to struggle over a beautiful golden-haired woman who is veiled in thin white gauze. She seems to glow with an inner light. They are threatening to kill Yossi and he tries to escape by swimming away on the surface of the water, but they can see him and shoot at him. Yossi returns to the near shore off to the left and finds two friends. He climbs onto their shoulders and dives into the water. At this point in the dream I replace Yossi, so that it is I who am swimming down, descending to the bottom of the lake. I swim farther and farther down finally reaching the mud at the bottom. I start to run out of air. I swim slowly to the top, and as I run out of air, I break the surface of the water. I look around me and realize that I am on the other shore, that I am safe and that I am home. I look around me as I walk out of the water and see a beautiful stone house set in the woods in the hills in front of me. I climb the path to the house. There are candles in the windows. I enter the house and see Yossi sitting at the table, where we sit and talk and eat, at peace.

That was the spring of 1972. I woke up from the dream and knew that I had found what I was looking for. I knew immediately that the dream was about being reinvigorated by the libidinal pool. But simultaneously it was religious, a retelling of the story, albeit in personal terms, of the Exodus event at the Red Sea. Suddenly it cast Judaism in a whole new light, as a tradition alive with at least one profound religious symbol. Exodus was no longer a political act but a symbol of rebirth and redemption from psychological and spiritual bondage.

From 'DESCENT INTO EGYPT' to 'GARDENING'

This essay described the process by which Dr Summergrad integrated his political, spiritual, and psychological interests. It utilized his dreams, events of his life, and memories of his involvement in meditation and religious experience.

A major insight that led to this integration was his recognition of the effect of disappointment. The rejection he experienced when he applied to college had a powerful effect on his self-esteem. This intense reaction led to a sequence of major alterations in his attitudes and personal activities. After a long and painful series of explorations of self, Zen, and personal isolation, he discovered much that is meaningful to him.

After the time described here, he went on to apply these recognitions to understanding similar threats to self-esteem in other people, especially to his patients. He was able to utilize his discoveries in strengthening his own concept of himself, and was, in turn, able to utilize that strength.

In the following essay, "Gardening," Dr Hamburg reflects upon a commonplace activity. He allows his mind to generate ideas and his thoughts to wander in a quest for his roots in relation to this activity. On the surface, this appears to be a rational, cognitive process, a profusion of ideas emanating from his activity, but the poetic imagery that appears so richly in his thinking and writing also reveals the involvement of emotional and intuitive processes.

Chapter 9

GARDENING

Paul Hamburg, M.D.

Take a piece of earth, enclose it, destroy the wild life it contains, turn over the soil and loosen it, enrich it with last year's cast-off growth, plant it, and you have a garden. You have entered into an ancient contract with creation to obtain nourishment through work.

You have reaffirmed a bond with time: rain and sun, warmth and frost, animal and plant, life and death. If you are an urban man, then there is little to take for granted in this act. From small, everyday actions emerges your place here on earth, your connection with your origins. In enclosing this space, fencing it to keep out wild animals, protecting the young plants, watching new growth, you are enclosing yourself, defining boundaries, revealing what culture has made obscure. In a more agricultural society these speculations would make no sense; the rhythm of work itself provides enough of a place in nature without any need for explication. But we have lost the possibility of spontaneous connection. While expanding our powers of consciousness, we contract. Returning to the garden, we confront an enigma: Can we enact this matrix of connection while retaining awareness of its meaning? The garden belongs to a world of spontaneous gesture that collides abruptly with the world of speculation.

A memory of 2000 years of exile is in my blood. My people have lost the sense of roots in a land; their land was the book. Their book was hope in the desert. Suspended between the pessimism of existence and a promise that ever receded into the future, they endured exile and worse. For generations, perched on the edge, ready to flee at a moment's warning, always wide-eyed, prepared to kindle sparks of conscience and questioning, they sought understanding. The view from beyond. Marginality was the source of perpetual curiosity, enigma, and poignance. Dispossessed long ago from the Garden and all gardens, unconnected with the source of nourishment and energy, united in the quest for return, the redemption of reclaiming, free of warlike possession, not rooted in place, free to speculate — this is the exile of my people from the land.

Gathered in cities that echo the barren desert, we lose touch with the soil. We eat, we become consumers, but we do not partake of origins. The cycle is broken. The act of consuming is broken off from the whole, separated from the collusion of sun, earth, and water with sweat. We eat and do not feel nourished; our hunger grows despite an elaboration of culinary art.

We work in the city and regard the sun's passage through the seasons as something apart from life, an object too far removed from any context that might restore the seasons to us or return us to our former place in the cycle of change.

So I chose to become a family doctor. I studied healing, seeking work that does not destroy. I ran away from the fortresses of technology that I found in the city, where ancient bonds of trust turned into hierarchies of alienation. As a country doctor I searched for the gaps that still allowed connection across the wall of instrumentality. I struggled against the force of separation that casts out the sick and dying to be invisible, alone, feared by the healthy, dominated by science. Somewhere near the margins of my profession, suspended between doubt and the patient's relentless demand for answers, I searched for a way to remain in touch.

Gradually, I learned that to tend a garden meant to return in some measure from each of these exiles, because gardening removed me from the remoteness of observing nature and allowed me to be at the center of a cycle of growth. It brought me back to the land from the city. It confronted me with the possibility of eating what I had helped grow.

To speak of the garden is to seize it at a particular moment in a cycle of change. Whether we see the garden as undulations of brown and gray, the tilled surface of potentiality, or as the outrageously varied greens of young growth — or as skeletal stems black upon a snowy surface in winter — we are seeing instants snatched away from streaks of continuous change.

Our affair with change may vary from anticipation (of the first seedling in the weeks after planting), to impatience (as we watch a favorite vegetable slowly ripen), to anxiety (as four rows of beans have matured simultaneously), to the bittersweet of regret — when the first frost has introduced the phase of fall decline.

Our awareness of growth will vary from straining to perceive the slowness of a plant's unfolding to the palpable expansion of the peak garden. Some changes are visible, a flash of color from a new flower, a row of new seedlings in a background of brown. Many changes remain unseen: new networks of roots seeking veins of water amidst the gravel deep underground, the cascade of genetic transcription that informs each plant in the garden, the bacterial transformations of nutrients in the soil. Sunlight is transfixed, the dryness of seeds moistened, dense life unfolds.

The garden changes with us, in us, by our activity and despite it. Caring for it establishes rhythms of involvement, draws us along in its own patterns, accelerations, hesitations. In its expansive growth and abrupt decline, the garden curves our experience; it forces us to notice its rhythm inside us.

I do not easily admit to violence in me.

Walking about for days with bright orange stains of potato beetles on my fingers, I avoid thinking I killed them. I think instead about new potatoes, how good they taste. A simple trade. In order to coax the potato plants to live long enough to make potatoes in the ground, I have to protect their leaves from young Colorado potato beetle grubs that hatch out every day. Every morning and every evening I go out to the garden and pick grubs, thousands of them. Some I squeeze between my fingers and some I drown in a glass jar, feeling a certain pleasure in watching the jar fill up with orange bodies. I do not like to recognize myself in this violence. The garden forces me to acknowledge my willingness to enter into a struggle for existence.

The first year I did not put up a fence, so the woodchucks came. As quickly as I could place young transplants in the garden the woodchucks ate them, leaving a bare stem, rows of bare stems. Sadness turned rapidly to anger, then rage. I remembered the gun my neighbor had asked me to keep for him when he was feeling depressed and unsure of himself. I spent hours staring at my garden from the kitchen window imagining that I saw my woodchuck enemy. I would run out with the shotgun ready to kill. Once finally, it was not my imagination; he was there sampling the newest transplants. I took aim, fired, fell down from the unexpected recoil, with an image of a furry ball flying in the air and landing with a thud on the ground. The fall from triumph to disgust took only a moment as I ran to the garden ready to administer first aid. I thought, "You're a lucky woodchuck, at least I'm a doctor." He was dead. I put him in the compost heap to join the garden at some later time.

Subtler forms of violence pervade gardening. I attack the sod, ripping it apart, tear into the soil, break it into powder, pull out a thousand weeds each week, constantly choosing what will live and what will die. I do not use poisons, preferring to remain responsible for my violence. There is death in every corner of the garden; it refuses to be relegated to the compost heap, to remain beyond the fence. Always, it enters the protected enclosure. Not able to dissect away the destruction, the death, from the life and nourishment, I learn something about myself.

This drive to contain, select, order, protect, perpetuate my own existence, enclosed itself within this garden, coupled with a willingness to permit growth to happen by itself, becomes tolerable. Perhaps we could deny it altogether, throw our seeds upon the meadow, hoping that an occasional one will penetrate the earth and grow, sharing the growth with other hungry creatures, making no claims of any entitlement. Perhaps we could survive this way, but there would be no garden. The garden is a compromise between accepting wildness and controlling nature, between the capacity for letting-be and the desire for mastery.

Such a coupling of our own masculinity and femininity carries profound implications. It accepts that creation consists both of a thrust into space and a withdrawal to make space for a new life. In this sense, the garden represents another return from exile, enabling each of us to feel in touch with our aggressiveness, uncomfortable as it is, and our capacity for allowing a new birth, unfamiliar as this might have become.

For weeks I have dreamt about this. Kept a nightly frost vigil. Every year at this moment the air fills with the same uneasy anticipation as darkness falls a little earlier each day, bringing a familiar yet strange aspect of cold into the space of evening. Every day I have harvested baskets of tomatoes, peppers, eggplants, of those vegetables whose long growing seasons just barely manage to squeeze into the short summer time. Surrounded by this production, I still cannot help anticipating the destruction that must soon arrive and sense the foreboding this knowledge brings to me.

One morning I wake to see that it has happened: Glassy, motionless silhouettes of icy plants outline the shape of my garden in a crystalline suspension between life and death. I walk out to see more. For another hour life will remain preserved under its icy transparent covering. Then green will turn to brown, juicy leaves and stalks will wither and wrinkle, the subtle shape of massive plants will crumble, herbs, beans, squash, cucumbers, tomatoes, peppers, corn will all be dead. The few islands of remaining life will stand out strangely among the drooping shades of the casualties. The broccoli, brussels sprouts, and cabbage will retain their life above the ground for many weeks to come; carrots will be alive beneath the ground for months. The rest of the garden is dead.

There are places I could have chosen to live where the growing season is longer. I think about them each year at this time and wonder whether I would be happier growing my garden there. And every year I come to the same conclusion. I decide that this is somehow preferable, this just marginally adequate span of time for the garden to be alive. It allows me each year to fill pantry and freezer with vegetables, feeding me and my family. The early frost is another, essential boundary of the garden, defining its value, even as it brings an ancient sadness each autumn.

The killing cold is part of the annual life of the garden, a death that permits next year's life. Each fall I find myself a little tired of the work. I walk around the garden, regretting an herb here and there that I neglected to harvest, reviewing the history of this year's growth, counting the richness of a present that has been transformed into the past. Nostalgia, sadness, anger, satisfaction, relief, all blend along with a respectful fear of the coming winter.

I often wondered what my place was in the garden. In some sense, my presence was essential. Without me there would have been no garden, just a wild meadow. It would have been a different kind of growth. Yet my importance did not include mastery, control, or domination of the garden. Rather, I was permitting growth, tending the plants, holding the framework that enabled the garden to unfold. The reflection of this work was my sense of being held and nourished. The type of knowledge that I acquired did not fall into the category of instrumental knowledge; I did not gradually learn to control or dominate. I learned instead about the realm of possibility within the life of the garden. I acquired the experience to allow me to know what to ask of the garden, to desire the possible. My own sense of power derived from a knowledge of the limitations of what I could realistically do. The boundaries of action defined a kind of freedom. If I became arrogant and planted vegetables with a long growing season, they froze; if I planted them too late they never matured; if I neglected the garden for some good reason, the weeds choked every other plant. Gradually I experienced the pleasure of knowing my place. Always there was a sense of acting-in-place-of another, in the way that Adam and Eve were asked to tend Eden. Participation in the annual cycle always renews this feeling of holding a place. And being held.

From 'GARDENING' to 'THE PAWN'

Dr Hamburg has shown us that much meaning could be found in an ordinary, everyday activity like gardening, if one troubles to examine it. He has the bent of a philosopher and the sensibility of a poet, qualities that not all of us possess. Yet, all of us can focus more actively on our ordinary activities and on the images and ideas that they generate. The key to it is to be alert and to capture them.

In the following presentation, Dr Scott Wilson uses a play in one act to present to us his search for meaning and direction.

Chapter 10

THE PAWN

Scott N. Wilson, M.D.

CAST: A Narrator, an Older Man, and a Younger Man. (At start of play, curtain is closed, and spotlight reveals narrator standing all the way stage right.)

NARRATOR: There's a crooked road that gnarls through each town and leads you by one or more hock shops, where, arrested by the promises of three spheres-of-plenty, you might cash in on your past. Or buy it off. Or try.

When you transact like that, it's never for the last time.

The color-flood of warm spring is barely enough to flesh out the stark outline of a young man. He is on just such a purposeful meander. Call him David. Call him John.

Of course, he finds the shop. (Lights up) There is a room, empty; the finish had come off the wooden walls. There is inevitable dust.

He enters and waits by the thick wire mesh that separates him from the pawnbroker, who listens silently to someone on the phone.

(There's a long pause during which the pawnbroker [Older Man] nods slowly.)

YOUNGER MAN: It's a long walk over here. . . .

OLDER MAN: You could've called. It saves some people a trip. (Then, to receiver:) No Ma'am. I can't help you. Goodbye. Yes?

YOUNGER MAN: I was wondering what I could get for this. (Takes ring out of pocket and hands it to Older Man through aperture in mesh.)

OLDER MAN: (Looks at ring) Ever do this before?

YOUNGER MAN: What?

OLDER MAN: Do you know what you're getting into?

YOUNGER MAN: What do you mean? What *AM* I getting into?

OLDER MAN: Well, look. Other day a young guy like you comes in—works at the hospital on Fifth Street. Day and night. Girlfriend doesn't see hide nor hair of him. Next thing you know, she breaks off the engagement.

YOUNGER MAN: (After long pause) So?

OLDER MAN: She gave him the ring back. He came in to pawn it.

YOUNGER MAN: Right . . . how much can I get for this? It cost me a fortune.

OLDER MAN: You sticking around these parts?

YOUNGER MAN: What business is that of yours?

OLDER MAN: Oh, none. None whatsoever. Only want to know whether you might be back for the ring someday. (Pauses) Probably not. You haven't got the look. Ten to one you'll be out of here in no time, like most young fellas. Here a few years, there a few years. If enough of 'em grew up and stuck around, this town would be overpopulated. I bet you wouldn't believe what they leave in my lap when they go.

YOUNGER MAN: Try me.

OLDER MAN: (Gets a frilly yellow dress that might fit a 10-year-old and holds it up for Younger Man to see) Cute, huh? Seems this guy played a girl's part in a school play when he was a kid. All boys' school. They made this dress to fit him—he wore it once, then it started collecting dust. It's still collecting dust. Wanna buy it? A dollar even.

YOUNGER MAN: I came here to get, not give.

OLDER MAN: Just kidding, Jack. Gave up trying to unload this thing ages ago. Well, at least someone might use it someday. Nobody'll ever use half this other crap. . .(Scans a shelf and his eyes light on something) Now here's something you'll want to snap right up. (Shows Younger Man a garish, absurdly designed tennis trophy) One of a kind! (Reads engraving aloud) "Runner-up, West Hartford Public Parks Boys' Doubles, 1970." Go for it.

YOUNGER MAN: Very funny.

OLDER MAN: Don't be that way. Somebody sweated bullets for this. You know what it cost in tennis lessons? Hundreds! Guy told me so himself. (Pauses, looks at Younger Man) For you, 75.

YOUNGER MAN: Look. I have something very valuable here. I need cash. How much will you give me?

OLDER MAN: (Looks at ring) Pretty big rock! Brand new mounting...18 carat gold. What'd you pay?

YOUNGER MAN: $750.

OLDER MAN: Must've meant a lot to you.

YOUNGER MAN: (Sarcastic) I worked late nights.

OLDER MAN: Not your money. Your woman must've meant a lot to you.

YOUNGER MAN: Oh, really? I suppose you have one of those back there, too...a woman, that is.

OLDER MAN: I'm going to have a tough time getting the story behind this ring. How do I know it isn't hot?

YOUNGER MAN: Hot? Do I look like a thief?

OLDER MAN: You sound like somebody who doesn't want to talk.

YOUNGER MAN: O.K. Fine. I had a deprived childhood. I grew up on Park Avenue. My father was a professor of theology, my mother was a dermatologist. But somehow we made ends meet.

I learned to know things about people that others couldn't see or appreciate. But I saw everything in terms of spirituality and skin. As I matured, I saw how useless this vision is in a world that is mainly concerned with money and power. I felt betrayed. I had to get out of there.

At 14, I left for boarding school. Four years later, college. I found I was not prepared to grapple with mundane problems. I raged at the world for ignoring spiritual problems so tangible to me. To be with others who thought the way I did, I attended a theological seminary. Those were days of struggle, days of learning. I gained self-knowledge, or so I thought. Through the study of beliefs, I grew to understand what drove people to do things. Or so it appeared. The world was in the palm of my hand! (Pauses) I fell in love and got engaged.

When I graduated from the seminary, I could find work only

in jobs that didn't interest me. I started going to night school. I worked weekends to pay my bills. My fiancee just gave me back the ring...right, she doesn't see me enough. (Pauses) If I can scrape together the loans, I might even make a new start, go to medical school, do something practical—

OLDER MAN: Hey, lookey here. (Shows Younger Man stethoscope, ophthalmoscope, and reflex hammer) Guy from Fifth Street Hospital up and decided to go into psychiatry—these are useless to him now. All yours for $15.

YOUNGER MAN: Let me think about it. (Impatiently) So what'll you give me for the ring?

OLDER MAN: (Scrutinizing) Where are you from?

YOUNGER MAN: New York. A plane ride away. Why?

OLDER MAN: I'll give you enough to get home.

(Curtain)

---

rom 'THE PAWN' to 'SURPRISE'

Internal conversations were presented by Dr Brotman; Dr Wilson externalizes the dialogue and presents it as an interaction between two characters, reflecting the influence of the past on the present, the interplay between work and personal life, and processes of separation and reunion. Even an ideal upbringing cannot anticipate all of the complexities that adult life can bring. Challenges, disappointments, and relationships arise that demand new responses.

Dr Summergrad's "failure" led to a tortuous path of development. The Younger Man intends to return home.

"The Pawn" gives us perspective on the experiences depicted by the author. At the same time, it produces an involvement of a special sort. It exemplifies the balance between detachment and involvement that characterizes significant insight. Immersion and detachment also characterize "Surprise." Dr Richard Rice presents a decade of sojourns in an Italian village.

Chapter 11

SURPRISE

Richard Rice, M.D.

Ten years ago my wife and I made our first trip to Italy. We have gone back every year since, but this year may have been our last. Our first trip was our honeymoon; we stayed from September through April. The dreams we brought and the experiences we found changed us both deeply. Now that we are different people, Italy too seems to have changed.

I was born in Miami, Florida, in 1940. I'm sure you've heard this before, but my upbringing was remarkable for its absences. I loved school in a way; it provided a structure I could hang on to. But I always knew something was missing within me. Sometime 10 or 12 years ago while I was in analysis and earning my living as an emergency room physician, I began to dream.

I dreamed that I would go away and find a beautiful place to live. I dreamed that I would do all the little things that I wanted to do, like walk and talk and just see what came. These were things I had squeezed in between my pressing responsibilities in school and work. I dreamed that if I could do these things and live in this place, I would find what had been missing all along. I know that many people have this dream sometime during their lives. But what made this dream special for me was that I was dreaming it, it was mine.

We were married in June, and we set off for Italy in September. We said good-bye to our whole life — family, friends, school, work, income, profession, and, as we were to learn, our American identity and the English language. We had $2500, clothing, and books. After a false start in Bolzano (the small goulash plate at lunch turned out to be only one meatball), we headed for Florence. We went to the information bureau in the train station and chose the area they didn't recommend, the Mugello Valley, 30 miles north of Florence. I had read that the people who lived in these hills, part of the Apennine Mountains, still lived in harmony with their natural surroundings.

We took a bus to the valley and began hitchhiking from town to town looking for a place to live. On the afternoon of the fourth day, as we were walking out of one town, I looked toward the sunlight, and there was the beautiful tip of the valley where the mountains began. I knew instantly we had found our place, that here was the place we would live. I asked an old man coming out of church and learned there was a small village out there. In fact, he said, his nephew was the butcher. For the next week we walked the three or four miles each way to the village and asked everyone we met if they knew of a house we could rent. There was no hotel or restaurant in the village; we stood out as strangers. My wife supplied the words from a dictionary and I spoke. We asked shopkeepers, people working in the fields, even children and the postman.

Finally the woman whose shop we went to every day to buy fruit for lunch said that maybe her father had a place and that she would introduce us. After work she took us a little way up a hill to the field next to her house and introduced us to a smiling handsome man in his late 70s. His name was Dino. He was a friendly, energetic guy with a wonderful face and sparkling eyes. He took us a little farther up the hill to where he and his family lived 15 years ago and showed us a three-room stone house, part of the original farmhouse. No one had lived in it for some years; there was corn drying on the floor. The next day Dino and I were sweeping the corn into sacks. We were home.

Our first task was to make our new home livable and respectable. The weather was cool and clear; the countryside looked like an Italian Renaissance painting. We cleaned and painted; we set up a bed and borrowed a table and refrigerator. I hooked up a wood-burning stove that was our only source of heat. We built shelves and pegs for our clothing and made curtains. Quickly my wife had to learn to shop, and we both had to learn to speak Italian. No one spoke English; the last Americans they had seen were soldiers in World War II. But I could see instantly in their eyes a look that said "you can do it" — Dino, his family, and others in the village.

They were hardworking, struggling farm people of independent character. They wished us well in a simple, direct, nourishing way. There was an enlivening spirit of cooperation and coexistence. Over the years they had learned ways of getting along together. In those first couple of months I was reduced to barely being able to speak or feed myself. I was frightened by a sense of loss I had rarely experienced before. My whole world was gone. But gradually filling its place was a secure, tangible feeling of standing with my own two feet on the ground, of dealing with the basics of life one day at a time and making it, of being held by and fed by the knowledgeable, caring people who knew and cherished life and wished us well. There were despairing moments — nothing ever works in Italy the first or second time, but we always knew we would make it, that we would be all right.

By the time winter came, we were in business. We could keep ourselves clean and almost warm; we could eat and sleep and manage our money; we could get along with each other some of the time. We looked forward to the weekly town hot shower on Saturday afternoon followed by a drink at the bar. We knew how to gather wild mushrooms and chestnuts and where to find wood for the stove. We knew when the market came to the neighboring town and how to shop there. I met a vendor at the market who gave us fish every Friday; we knew a waiter who never charged us for second helpings. We began visiting our neighbors after supper; this is an old farm custom called "a veglia." We listened to stories of the Germans and Americans during the war, of work, of work in the mines and fields before and after the war, of everyday life in the village, and of family members and events 2, 10, and 50 years ago. We sat around the kitchen table by the fire and heard about current work, feudal life before the war, about mean stepparents who kept the bread under lock and key, and about courtship, survival, and death in the woods.

Our friends were good storytellers; there were tears and laughter and heated debate between grandfather and grandson about the age of the universe and the direction of Genoa. By 9 or 10, we washed it all down with warm milk and coffee, lit our flashlights, and said good night. These evenings were giant doses of plain old-fashioned human interaction. There was no abstract thinking or planning for the distant future. There was a lot of give and take, right out on the table. Before I knew it, I was involved with and in love with people and families more than I had been for a long, long time. These feelings of contact, connection, belonging, acceptance, knowing, and caring felt new and nourishing to me. I hadn't found time or place for these feelings in the long years of medical school and internship; I had forgotten they were missing. I didn't go to Italy to find them; they were a surprise! But they were as exciting and wonderful as my growing sense of surviving on my own. I believe each experience enhanced the other.

There are hundreds and hundreds of stories, trips, hikes, adventures, meals, and people I would like to tell you about. Every day was full, rich, exciting with many successes and failures. By the time April came we knew everybody and everything, or at least we felt we did. I had a greater sense of personal accomplishment that came from within than I ever had before. I had learned a tangible appreciation for living life one day at a time. We had made a life for ourselves that felt good! Leaving was terrible; we were torn from our lives there. We both had school to begin, but weren't ready to leave. We've often wondered what our lives would be like had we stayed.

For the past nine years we've returned every summer to the same village for one or two months. There was never a question about going back. We felt grounded and rooted there. We needed to go back to pick up where we had left off, to continue what was so important to us and felt so good. We got to know more families, more grandparents, and many new babies. The foreignness between us began to lift, and we began to see and know each other more openly. Our speaking improved. We began to understand what was behind their words. We began to fit into their lives as they did and feel comfortable doing so. I felt the whole town as a living, social organism. The interconnections among people were infinite. I felt the security and after several years, the restrictions of this structure. After 5 or 6 years, we also learned about feuds that had gone on for 20 years, sometimes between brothers. We weren't just guests anymore; our closest friends shared both sides of their lives. I loved just hanging around with the guys in the piazza. I felt I was being myself. I didn't know how to be anything else, and they would have seen through it. Every August we took part in the festa. My wife cooked for three days, and I sold sausages for three nights to locals and Florentines on country outings. Our relationship with the town culminated two summers ago when, during the festa, we were called up on stage and awarded honorary citizenship. There was quite a moving ceremony where a friend talked about our years there and about life in a village for everyone. He quoted a line from a poet, "To live in a village is to be not alone."

During the first few years of this story, I was a psychiatry resident in Boston. My experiences in Italy helped me to see quickly that even the sickest patients were still people. And as people, they too could survive. The positive attitude, the respect, and understanding of life and survival I learned from the people in Italy helped me as I sat and struggled with my patients. I believe I was able to communicate some of this hopeful attitude to them in a way that was useful. After school in Boston, we moved to a town in western Massachusetts to begin living and working on our own. It's something of the people in Italy, of Dino, and of some people in Boston that has helped us get started out here and survive the rough spots. That sense that something's missing is gone now. Instead I feel a reaching out, an attachment, a capacity.

The year I turned 40 was a crisis for me, the economy was down, my practice was slow, I had to struggle to survive. Even before leaving for Italy I was vaguely less enthusiastic about going. I felt a slight tinge of returning out of obligation, not just desire. After a few days in the village, it was clear that something had changed. On their part, they were a little older. Especially Dino, now 86, seemed to be slowing down. And friends we used to take hikes with were now busy taking care of their children. I felt a bit like a stranger. Some slight thing that had been was gone, lost, had disappeared. My feelings for them were unchanged, but I wasn't just their child anymore. I was going through the motions. My thoughts kept returning to our home in America. I imagined my apartment, my wife's garden, my work, and our friends. I longed to be home, not because home was better, but because that's where I belonged. New roots were awakening within me and, like my wife's plants, they sought the soil in their own back yard.

So this is leaving and losing. They've given me so much and now I'm turning away. Not right, not fair, shouldn't have to be! But inside, it is right. The very life that was awakened within me says it's right, essential.

I went to Italy to live my dream, maybe my second childhood. I'm happy I did. But the surprise was all the personal connection and sharing. The confidence, the urge to get on with my life comes from them. Yet this same urge requires that I turn away from them. I see that we don't just leave bad homes, but we leave good homes too. It's not an empty, lonely feeling, but a full sadness of losing them.

Where do we go from here? I'm going to learn to speak Italian more fluently. I'll find time to visit them during the year, maybe in winter when they have less work and more time at home. It will be different between us; their own kids don't do this; growing up doesn't mean moving out. But they're a part of us now and we cherish them. Hopefully, we'll still be able to share our feelings with them, even from a position of greater independence. I think the chances are pretty good; they've been working things out for a thousand years in that little village.

From 'SURPRISE' to 'ON LOSING A PATIENT'

The themes of loss, separation, intimacy, and degrees of closeness are pervasive in human life. They are, accordingly, prominent in psychiatric work. It is natural that these themes are also essential in the personal lives of psychiatrists. In "Surprise," the village is not merely geographically removed from familiar surroundings in Miami or in Boston. Dr Rice and his wife entered the village as strangers from another country, but made human connections from the very beginning and developed relationships with many of the people they encountered. They were gradually included in the social life of the village.

His acquaintance with the language, the customs, and the individual members of that village grew gradually stronger, deeper, and closer. Eventually he separated from the village as he became more involved in a new community in western Massachusetts, where he settled with his wife, and where he opened his private practice. He had learned that he as an individual, and he and his wife as a couple, were able to establish a home in a far-away place, and build from the rudiments.

His experience also helped him to deal with another kind of foreignness. The latter appeared in some of his sicker patients. He was able to make connections with them in ways that were far more meaningful than had been possible for him prior to his involvement in the Italian village. As he became able to move away from the familiar into the new, he was able to develop his independence as well as to continue his connections with the past.

In all of this, he developed a perspective that enabled him to look at his own development as a continuous sequence of experience. He could see his own life unfolding in terms of leaving home to enter into his educational experience, then to the experience in Italy, and eventually to the establishment of an independent household and a professional practice.

Dr Stephen Kleinman, in "On Losing a Patient," helps us to look at another aspect of closeness, emotion, attachment, and separation.

Chapter 12

ON LOSING A PATIENT

Stephen Kleinman, M.D.

The first time I met Ms D. I thought she might be psychotic. She jumped quickly from one thought to another, an apparently disconnected discourse on her religiousness, her sinfulness, her left-wing politics, her previous therapy, and her mother's ruthlessness and possible sexual abuse. I stopped her for a moment with a question, which I needed to do as much for me as her since the room was whirling around for both of us after a few minutes of her stream of whatever it was. Disconcertingly, she came to an abrupt stop. She said nothing, looking as if my question itself had forced her to realize that she could talk fast but not think at all. This apparent thought blocking, the hard-to-follow content of her thoughts, and the intensity of her large protuberant eyes worried me. Was she paranoid? Did her religious conversation represent a psychotic world in which she was bombarded with bizarre thoughts? Should I hastily retreat from the in-depth interview? Should I switch to a concrete, present-oriented approach, searching for specific delusions, hallucinations, or paranoid thoughts, trying to find the right drug to allow her to organize her thinking?

From the beginning there was something about her I liked, a sincere interest in digging out the reasons behind the anxiety she often felt. This glimmer of sincerity persuaded me to join with her in exploratory psychotherapy. I tried to put aside my fears of her imminent breakdown and help her understand the forces that had brought her to this point.

The therapy lasted five months. It was always hard because she so intensely scrutinized everything, but she did reasonably well. She found herself able to go home over Christmas and not fight with her mother for the first time in years. During our sessions she showed less thought blocking and more coherence. She always seemed fragile, just one step from falling apart. The better I came to know her, the more I felt she suffered from a particularly frightening kind of anxiety with which she somehow always managed to cope. She never called between sessions and always came on time. Almost continually she worried that she might be only a step away from the state hospital. She questioned everything about herself, felt ugly, felt stupid, felt that she might be an emotional leech (her mother's phrase). She feared she might never find a career in journalism but be forced to languish forever in her quasi-secretarial job.

However, she did have an ability to put her fears in some perspective, even to laugh at some of them. As I became aware of this ability, I viewed therapy as being able to help this frightened woman develop rewarding relationships. She began to see that she was not to blame for all she felt responsible about. Even on her worst days she managed to endure. I felt gratified. The therapy was working well, and our relationship as therapist and patient had the feeling of being a cooperative venture.

Then one day she told me that, to her amazement, the newspaper she most wanted to work for—to which she had previously applied and been rejected—had an editorial job opening. The newspaper was in a different city, and if she did get the job it would, of course, mean ending therapy. As it turned out she was hired, leaving us with only one session prior to her departure to end our relationship.

It was difficult for me. In fact, I liked her a great deal and cared for her. And now, suddenly, this remarkable venture was over. We were parting, and I did not want to say good-bye. There were so many other patients with whom I did not have the attachment I had toward her. Why didn't they leave instead? Why not one of the much longer therapies that had floundered and that I could not find a way to make more vital? I was losing someone I did not want to lose, even though our relationship was nothing beyond patient and therapist.

There was the crux of my dilemma. Could I tell Ms D. that I liked her a great deal, that indeed I would miss her? Although I realized the new job was what she really wanted, I really hated to see her go. "I'm really very sad to see you go, Ms D.," I imagined myself saying to her as she told me that this would be her last session. Can a therapist say such a thing and still be acting professionally?

Prior to my experience with Ms D. I had a fairly straightforward approach to the end of therapy. I would elicit all that I could about the patient's thoughts and feelings on ending therapy, and then I would tell the patient how I thought things had gone, wish the patient luck, and shake hands good-bye. But I had to struggle with a desire to tell Ms D. how I felt about her and her therapy. I had to balance this impulse against the natural vulnerability patients feel in response to any pronouncement by the therapist, especially with the particular sensitivity of Ms D., whose mother had often been cruelly critical of her. I wanted to tell her only that I liked her, found her not at all to be the "parasite" her mother frequently called her, and that I felt further treatment could help her resolve more of her difficulties.

Eventually, I did tell her how I felt. I told her I found her to be a very nice person who was making an earnest and successful effort to place her world in a perspective that would allow her to be less depressed and anxious. I also told her that in opposition to her mother's sometime view of her as a "parasite," I found her considerate of others much of the time. When she finally did get up to leave, I reached out to shake her hand, but she bypassed this gesture to embrace me in the manner of someone saying good-bye to a close friend. I accepted this, hugging her in return. Then she left.

There is nothing so extraordinary about Ms D.'s case, but for me the explicit sense of liking her and feeling quite sad at her leaving had a resonance that I had not previously experienced. It caused me to focus on how to deal with positive, even loving feelings about a patient who abruptly decides to leave. Before Ms D., it seemed to me that it was angry feelings that were the really tough ones, that liking someone was not a problem as long as reasonable therapeutic distance was maintained. Her case led me to recognize some possibilities I had been unaware of about being a psychotherapist.

It is an odd, detached stance that one assumes in psychotherapy. There are times when I want the protection of the psychotherapeutic shield, times I've found it both personally helpful and therapeutically useful, for instance, in people with overly eroticized notions about me, or vice versa, or in people whose hostility, ego boundaries, or paranoid proclivities are in poor control. It is both a relief and a necessity to establish enough distance. There needs to be a clear focus on what therapy is supposed to accomplish. I think the episode with Ms D. raised the issue that we sometimes go too far in the establishment of this distance, at least in the insistence that it persist right through difficult leave-takings.

Most of all, this case has left me to reflect on the personal "cost" of being a psychotherapist. The intimacy and detachment that mark this venture make considerable demands to restrain oneself from proclaiming too many opinions or deepest feelings. Since Ms D.'s departure, I have begun to reconsider the tight bounds by which we operate. They are usually necessary, but not always. Although I had dealt with this issue in a general way previously, Ms D. led me to take these ideas and make them far more vital. I've become less apt to accept the set rules or notions of the lore of psychiatry and more willing to disclose some of my feelings to certain patients, when good judgment and my intuition reasonably coincide.

From 'ON LOSING A PATIENT' to 'SONG ASSOCIATIONS'

Dr Kleinman was surprised to discover that Ms D. was more significant to him than he had suspected. He recognized his affection for her. In a highly responsible, professional way, he hesitated before revealing warm feeling for the patient, until he had time to think through the consequences. He was aware that an expression of attachment might be as burdening to the patient as it can be in other relationships. He was careful not to say something that might harm the patient—restraint characteristic of the physician who is dedicated to do no harm.

While caution and consideration are duties of the professional, they can be exercised in social and personal relationships as well. Dr Kleinman was explicitly aware of his duty to the patient. Comparable duties exist between people who are related socially or personally.

This essay illustrates an autognostic sequence that can be followed by others in or out of the medical profession. It begins with recognition of a strong feeling, followed by a period of reflection and inner examination, with action deferred. In this case, the action consisted of vocalization of his feelings. Finally, the sequence led to a change in attitudes and in modification of subsequent behavior.

The next essay, "Song Associations," describes autognostic sequences that begin with music that comes to the mind of the therapist during treatment sessions. The sequences then lead to emotional experience, to greater empathy, and to more clinically effective understanding.

Chapter 13

SONG ASSOCIATIONS

Marie Armentano, M.D., and
Michael S. Jellinek, M.D.

It is a well-accepted principle that psychotherapists should be aware of their own thoughts and feelings while listening to the patient. In our development as therapists, we have noticed that occasionally songs come to mind while we are with our patients; sometimes a melody or fragment, other times a whole song. We have found that examining those musical associations has proven helpful in much the same way as the exploration of other associations such as our own or the patient's memories and dreams. We will present two examples of our song associations as therapists and their usefulness in treatment.

CASE 1

Jessica is an attractive 15 year old who entered treatment at the urgent request of her family and school. She was the oldest of three children who grew up in a home with a demanding father who was himself frustrated in his career and a mother who was seen as distant, and recently, hostile. Despite her superior intelligence, Jessica had performed very inconsistently in her local school and continued this trend when she transferred to a boarding school. Her parents were worried about her overall lack of achievement and direction. In addition, there was evidence of promiscuity as well as a series of phone calls from the boarding school stating that Jessica was "in trouble," depressed, isolated, and "making up stories."

Therapy had proceeded slowly due to cancellations and Jessica's vague and distant manner of relating. During the 15th session, Jessica appeared especially sad and anxious. She was about to fail at school, unable to concentrate, and had told her schoolmates several false stories about being pregnant, having cancer, and the like. When gently confronted she told of her inner turmoil; of her inability to decide what "front" to use, unsure why she was lying; and of feeling mistrustful and profoundly alone.

As the intensity of her feelings increased, the therapist started to hear a song with the following lyrics:

> *Know me by the light, of a fire shining bright*
> *Know me by your bed where I have laid*
> *Know me and you might, if just for a night*
> *You'll know me by no other name*
> *Some girls will bring you silver*
> *Some will bring you fine Spanish lace*
> *Some will say I love you*
> *Some will have my face*
> *Some will bring you gold, and babies to hold*
> *I bring you only pain*
> *You can know me if you will by the wind on the hill*
> *You'll know me by no other name*
> *Some girls will die for money, some will die as*
> *   they are born*
> *Some will swear they die for love,*
> *Some die every morn*
> *I'll die alone, away from my home*
> *Nobody knows where I came*
> *The stone at my head will say I am dead*
> *It knows me by no other name.*[1]

The particular lyrics that repeated in the therapist's mind were "Know me by the light of a fire shining bright. You'll know me by no other name." These words captured what Jessica was saying — that her inner sense of self was a lonely shadow. She could shine brightly by putting up a front, but she remained anonymous.

Hearing these lyrics made the therapist stop an intellectual effort to differentiate "identity confusion" from character diagnosis and be able to feel intensely sad and anxious. Almost immediately, the therapist began listening empathically and feeling the depth of Jessica's loneliness. In thinking about the song later, the therapist remembered that many times he had played it as a college sophomore and remembered the identity conflicts of his own late adolescence.

CASE 2

Peter is a 31-year-old single man who had been in therapy for three years. His initial complaint had been chronic depression and crippling interpersonal anxiety. Although bright and motivated, he was sometimes a discouraging patient because of his extreme sensitivity to disappointment and his difficulty relaxing in the sessions. When discouraged because he felt criticized or that he wasn't communicating properly, he would become so anxious that he would ramble or remain silent. He would experience attempts to draw him out as critical demands, yet if the therapist was silent, he felt abandoned. Much of the time, although the therapist knew he was in pain, she was unable to listen empathically; her strongest feelings were irritation and frustration. After the patient attempted a new course of study and then dropped it because of his anxiety, he became increasingly depressed so that he was unable to work in therapy or at his job. Because of concerns about his expressed hopelessness and suicidality, therapist and patient had agreed on hospitalization.

During an interview on the ward, Peter was feeling better and was able to use the time to reflect on his past, something he hadn't been able to do in a long while. Both the patient and therapist were in a relaxed, receptive mood probably because the burden of worrying about management issues was lightened. The patient began talking about his mother, who had suffered from a schizoaffective disorder and who had been depressed and psychotic at frequent intervals throughout his childhood. He had begun to discuss his affection for her and his feeling that he was like her. When asked how he was like her, he began talking about how they were both too "gentle for this world." At this moment the therapist noted that she was mentally humming Don McLean's song "Vincent," a beautiful, sad song about Vincent Van Gogh's suicide that includes the following words:

> *Starry, starry night*
> *Paint your palette blue and grey*
> *Look out on a summer's day*
> *With eyes that know the darkness in my soul...*
> *And when no hope was left in sight, on that starry,*
>   *starry night,*
> *You took your life, as lovers often do;*
> *But I could have told you, Vincent, this world was*
>   *never meant for one as beautiful as you.*[2]

The affect was sadness and tenderness. The therapist realized how closely this patient identified with his mother and how protective he felt of her and of himself. He saw himself and his mother as delicate and fragile. It occurred to the therapist that this depression might constitute an identification with her, his weak, delicate mother, who was, he felt, too beautiful and delicate for this world. His father, in contrast, was perceived as harsh and abusive. With encouragement, he elaborated on the theme that in order to survive in this world you needed to be insensitive. In his view of life, he conceived two mutually exclusive paths: to be harsh, insensitive, and survive, or to be gentle and loving, and, hence, to perish. Peter had chosen his mother's path.

The song helped the therapist appreciate Peter's feelings toward his mother and thus served as an affective bridge to this hard-to-reach patient. The therapist always found the song especially poignant and sad; in medical school a teacher had related the history of a patient whose son had committed suicide. The patient had associated to this song and burst into tears. In addition, the therapist's father's name is Vincent, and the song reminds her of her parents. The intensive repetitive associations to the song in the presence of Peter served to deepen an affective appreciation of his distress.

Although we cite only two examples, we have had numerous other experiences in which listening to songs that come to mind has helped to break through to a more empathic understanding of the patient. Rather than viewing this phenomenon as an annoying interruption to our concentration, we have tried to use it as an opportunity for enrichment of understanding. In the cases described, the therapist was frustrated with the patient and was coping with frustration through nonproductive intellectual effort. Listening to the song associations and attempting to understand them changed the mood in both therapy hours from one of frustrated nonunderstanding to one of empathic bridging. In both cases the therapist went from an anxious, intellectual, cognitive state to a relaxed, musing reflective state. The patient, sensing the changed climate of the hour, also seemed to participate more fully in the interaction and the sessions became rich and productive.

In looking at all the songs to which we associate, it is clear that they must have some personal significance to the therapist. Having associations that reverberate with those of the patient can make the therapist feel closer to the patient, to see the patient less as a separate creature to be analyzed and more as a fellow human being who shares human sorrows and joys, a phenomenon that results in some breakdown of ego boundaries between the patient and therapist and allows for closeness. Although the internal musing about the melodies and lyrics, the wandering through private associations, might be a regression, it is regression in the service of the empathic elements of the therapist.

REFERENCES

1. Stoakey P: *No Other Name*, Album 1700.
2. McLean D: *Vincent*. New York, Mayday Music and the Benny Bird Co., 1971, 1972.

From 'SONG ASSOCIATIONS' to 'DISCREDITED FEELINGS RECALLED'

The metaphor of interpersonal distance may facilitate interaction between people. Degrees of intimacy are difficult to measure. One indication of closeness is the experience of kind, sympathetic, tender feelings that incline one to reach out to embrace the other person. Aversion impels one to become more separate.

The song about the light evoked in the therapist sadness and anxiety. Experiencing these emotions helped to counteract the intellectual activity that had been separating them. The reader can infer that sadness and anxiety helped the therapist to get in touch with what the patient was experiencing. This permitted more complete understanding of the patient's experience.

The song of "Vincent" evoked feelings of sadness and tenderness in the therapist. As the authors mentioned in their discussion, the songs enabled the therapist to "break through to a more empathic understanding of the patient." They recognized the richness and usefulness of this form of contact with the inner experience of the patient. The therapists found that it led to optimal therapeutic distance.

Although this process was discerned in psychotherapy, it occurs in other relationships if such perceptions can enrich and deepen understanding. Often, intense emotions are hidden, insulated, and kept out of consciousness. Numerous conduits can make these inner wells of feeling accessible. In "Discredited Feelings Recalled," Dr Ellen Andrews tells how autognosis enabled her to tap into anger and attitudes about feminism that she had managed to keep out of her awareness for a long time.

Chapter 14

DISCREDITED FEELINGS RECALLED

Ellen Andrews, M.D.

Early in medical school I heard good doctors are good observers. I had worked hard to become just that, but what became apparent during the autognosis seminar was that I had been systematically ignoring one entire field of perceptions, "negative" affects such as anger. While I could make careful observations, I had a low threshold for discrediting them.

The thrust of the autognosis seminar was to think actively about how it felt to become a doctor and a psychiatrist. The advantages were several. There was explicit shared recognition that becoming a psychiatrist represented a real change and generated confusion, excitement, and apprehension. This was important because I had assumed that any confusion I felt must be unique to me and due to some fault of mine to be kept secret. Noticing such feelings had a specific purpose. Addressing such conflict did not result in chaos and destruction as I had always been taught. That this process offered me so much personally while making me a better physician seemed elegantly efficient. The result was relief from isolation and excitement about whole new areas opening up.

While the seminar is part of psychiatric training, it is something that all physicians could use to advantage, but unfortunately, elsewhere in medicine there is pressure opposite to what is taught in the seminar. Many physicians measure their skill in terms of how little they are affected by feelings in their work. They ignore personal reactions to the extraordinary variety of situations encountered. There is the inevitable tendency to like some patients more than others. There are unlimited variables in the ways we can affect each other in a physician-patient relationship. With some patients this can lead to increased empathy, while other patients arouse antipathy. Without specific instruction about how this occurs and what to do about it, there is potential for harm at worst, and for diminished effectiveness at best. Beyond the obvious interaction, there is the history that each person inevitably brings. When doctors ignore this, they get swept up in confusing situations and wonder what happened. Unaware of their own needs, they manipulate patients to provide things for them, in effect reversing roles. When there are many difficult and demanding patients to be seen, one "nice" patient can be encouraged to provide comfort to the physician, who may in turn ignore that patient's needs.

Aware of such a process, one can then analyze and learn from it, possibly avoiding it in the future. The usual process for most physicians, though, is to be relatively unaware of it, since the training emphasizes and even reinforces neglect of one's own feelings about patients, particularly negative feelings. Thus, the seminar was useful in reversing that habit of neglect. Gradually, I was learning another definition of a good doctor: not simply someone who loves patients, but someone who takes good care of them despite negative or positive personal feelings.

The pitfall alluded to earlier is this: making good observations but then discrediting them. It may seem paradoxical that a seminar for psychiatrists could be based on such an obvious principle, but making observations and generating hypotheses to explain them is the universal process of all science and medicine. The most dangerous mistake is to reject data that do not fit, when instead we should generate new hypotheses.

Consider the case of an elderly woman presenting with a complaint that her bowels haven't worked for three weeks. The doctor can choose to disbelieve her and assume she is unreliable or try to imagine what could possibly explain that complaint, however preposterous it sounds. It could lead to serious harm if the doctor discredits her story, but to explain it will require some effort and reorganization of thinking. Similarly, a patient might report sexual advances made by another physician. Again, one can either discredit the report of the patient, or one can open one's mind to new and troubling hypotheses to explain it.

I recently had a difficult case in which I noticed one laboratory value that seemed out of line. None of the other doctors had mentioned it, and since I did not perceive myself as an expert in that field, I decided it must be of no consequence or that it would be easily understood had I known more about that field. I had fallen into the trap of discrediting myself and discarding an observation. That particular piece of information was the key to the whole case. Once someone else called attention to it, everything fell into place. The person who did so was a better observer than I since he did not discredit his observation.

Acknowledging intolerable feelings and not discrediting good observations apply to areas of life other than medicine. I realized during the seminar that I had systematically ignored something else: my reaction to the women's movement. It had coincided with college and medical school, but I had neatly sidestepped it. Other women had formed support groups, but I had been rather suspicious and scornful of them. I wondered what their problem was, since I had not noticed any harassment or discrimination, any offensiveness or isolation.

I think it was no coincidence that when I finally became open to these questions during the seminar, it may have been the overdue erosion of my tendency to discredit the observations of other women that made this possible. Once opened to this, I experienced a cascade of new things. I was learning a great deal from and about other women, including patients, which relieved some of the isolation I had felt. It reassured me that my own feelings, ignored or explained away over the years, were legitimate and were shared and recognized by others. I could then inquire about such things in patients, having confidence that they would know what I was talking about; they would be relieved that someone finally had asked about and acknowledged their struggles. It was staggering to realize to what extent I had been ignoring conflicts about gender issues. I felt guilty about the patients I must have seen and never asked about incest, violence, job harassment. I was forced to examine my own stereotypes about seductive and hysterical women. I was horrified to realize how prone I was to hear of a rape and to think in very traditional terms about the woman involved.

Dealing with anger has been one of the most difficult lessons of all. I am gradually learning to what extent women repress their anger, and to what lengths women will go to avoid others' anger. I have had to become aware of how uncomfortable I am when a patient is angry with me. I have to watch what strategies I use to deflect it, ignore it, devalue it, "explain" it. I have to acknowledge the impact of my actions on the patient and how they have reinforced what others had done to her in the past and to change this sequence so that she could express anger and so I could at last hear it.

The autognosis seminar was a window on a world of new experience, namely, acknowledging feelings, even unpleasant ones, and learning useful things to do with them. It was the end of a long isolation from other people and from women in particular. If I could have continued the autognosis discussions, there are some things I would like to have taken up. There are many parallels between the women's movement and the denigration of psychiatrists by other medical specialists. There could have been fascinating discussions about analogous reasons for both. I can only speculate why this didn't take place. Maybe collectively we were all discrediting important observations, despite our best efforts not to.

From 'DISCREDITED FEELINGS RECALLED' to 'AN EXPERIENCE OF ILLNESS'

Dr Andrews emphasizes that physicians are trained to minimize, or even to neglect entirely, personal feelings about patients. She adopted that attitude and not only diminished her own feelings, but discredited her observations outside. Her recognition of perceptual denial opened her to feelings she previously overlooked. These included attitudes about women's issues.

Crumbling denial opened new areas of emotion and sensitivity. She became less isolated, more enthusiastic about important areas of professional and personal life. Dr Andrews' attention to her resistances led to major insights. This is parallel to psychotherapy, in which understanding of defenses leads to new knowledge at deeper levels of personality.

Her essay also demonstrates that there is often a discrepancy between what one knows and what one feels. This intelligent, highly trained, and competent physician knew many women had strong feelings about feminist issues. Yet she had felt isolated and estranged from other women and from her inner self.

Her essay also illustrated the value of revealing attitudes and emotions to compassionate people. Drives, fantasies, and reactions can be condemned inwardly as strange or shameful while they are hidden. When they are revealed, they can be re-evaluated and accepted. As a person becomes reconciled with his or her "discredited" emotions, new opportunities for personal growth and emotional development are born.

In the next essay, Dr Marie Armentano tells us how the experience of illness enabled her to recognize defenses. She discovered that insulation against feelings of vulnerability and helplessness had served to create impediments to understanding patients.

Chapter 15

AN EXPERIENCE OF ILLNESS

Marie Armentano, M.D.

It is late on a summer Wednesday afternoon. I am standing with a colleague when I feel a sharp pain, so severe that I press my abdomen with one hand and my face changes. He asks me if I'm all right and I say I don't know. The pain lessens a bit—I smile and say "I must have had about six cups of coffee today; the last one must have done it. I'll go borrow some Mylanta." We finish talking, I get the Mylanta and forget it. Halfway through my next patient, the pain returns; during the next hour it gets worse. Now I begin to worry.

I don't usually let myself think about anything going wrong with my body. When I get a bad cold and my cervical nodes swell, flickering thoughts about Hodgkin's disease are pushed down fast; in order to function day to day, I can't get that frightened. But when the worry begins, it comes with a force and intensity that are overwhelming.

I am alone in an office at the hospital. Just about everyone is gone for the day. I suddenly double over. I lie down on the floor. What the hell am I doing on the floor? I'm supposed to be functioning. It was three hours ago. What is it? Is this what an acute abdomen is like? I remember reading Sir Zachary Cope in medical school. It is vital that I remember—appendicitis? A perforated viscus? What if it gets worse? What if I can't get up? I get up.

It's probably nothing. What if I go down to the emergency

room and there's nothing wrong? They'll think I'm a crock—they already think psychiatrists are weird. I don't want them to think I'm a hypochondriac. So, now I've gotten up, I'll just go home. I'll be all right. As the pain wanes I dismiss it; as it waxes I worry. I'm afraid to go home, I live alone: What if there's really something wrong and there's no one to help me. Stupid, you're at a great hospital, what better place to be sick? You're going to go home? What if you have to come back? But I don't want to overreact—Italians aren't supposed to be very good with pain. I don't want to be hysterical. I want to be reasonable.

Finally, I go downstairs and get the attention of the clinic secretary at the walk-in medical clinic rather than the emergency room. I check in and am told to wait. It is cold in the hall. The pain lessens. I begin to feel ridiculous. I am annoyed at waiting. I don't want to waste my time—most of all I don't want some other doctor to think I'm wasting his time. I remember the contempt in which I held crocks. Terrible to be one. I am about to get up when I'm called in. The nurse takes my vital signs and asks about my chief complaint. I try to convey my reasonableness, but I am embarrassed when my vital signs are normal. The doctor who sees me is young and serious. He takes a careful history and examines me, asks me more closely about the aspirin I have been taking for headaches. My relief at being taken seriously is followed by alarm. He thinks I have gastritis from too much aspirin, but he is talking about migraines and electroencephalograms. I feel suddenly guilty about taking all that aspirin and drinking all that coffee, just like I do when I must confess to the dentist that I haven't been flossing. Like it's all my fault—like my health is a loan and I've been delinquent on the payment.

Migraine! I don't want migraine, I want little tension headaches. I wouldn't be caught dead having an electroencephalogram —all that paste in my hair. What if they find something? There are some questions I'd rather not ask. I might get an answer. The episode ends with advice to take Tylenol instead of aspirin, and antacids for a few days, and to come back in a week if I'm still having pain. I take about three doses of Mylanta, and then I forget it and go back to my life. After a few days it's hard to believe that I felt what I did.

Why is it that the experience of illness is so quickly forgotten? I am struck by the dichotomy of my experience of illness as the doctor and then as the patient; there seems to be a wall between. I remember as a medical intern, my anger and exasperation at my patients who seemed "unreasonable" about their illnesses: The 50-year-old married woman who clutched at my arm and cried when I tried to tell her about the bronchoscopy we wanted to do to see whether the mass in her lung was a malignant carcinoma or benign granuloma. She wouldn't listen; sometimes she'd cover her ears. And there she was coughing more and growing thinner day by day—why wouldn't she let us really help her? I could appreciate intellectually that she must be very frightened, but I wished she was smart. There was the obese 60-year-old man with heart failure and emphysema I found smoking a day after his transfer from the cardiac care unit. He'd been treated for the third time for pulmonary edema—and here he was, smoking a cigarette in the hall. And the 40-year-old male alcoholic with terminal ascites whom I found buying six bags of salty potato chips at the vending machines. What was wrong with these people? Didn't they realize what they were doing to themselves? Isn't it enough that we have to deal with bacteria and viruses and human cells gone wild? Must my patients actually collaborate with their enemies?

I am especially sobered when I realize that when I am the patient, I don't fulfill my own criteria, as a physician, for good patienthood. If I were to describe the events with which I begin this, I might use words unconnected with myself—hypochondria, denial, and noncompliance. As the patient, however, things look different.

I go a little crazy when I think I'm ill—what, in my role as a psychiatrist, I would call regressing. All of a sudden, as the patient, I am not in control. The belief that nothing can go wrong completely evaporates, the spectre of death appears, the prospect of pain and disfigurement. I am frightened, I need someone to help me, to tell me what to do, to tell me everything will be all right. At the same time I am fearful I will be hurt. Maybe it is all a nightmare, maybe if I refuse to believe it, it will go away. As a physician, my appreciation of the experience of illness is intellectual. As a patient, it is personal.

Empathy is the awareness (including the meaning and significance of the feelings) of the emotions and behavior of another person. Psychiatrists need to empathize with their patients in much of their work, and I have been able to do so in many situations. Why the lack in this area? As I look around at my colleagues, I begin to suspect that I am not the only one who has encountered this difference.

A woman tells me about her sudden loss of vision in a quadrant of her visual field, finally diagnosed as migraine. She describes having a CAT scan: She felt totally vulnerable as she was tied down, it was like being fed into a saw at a sawmill. She too describes the alternating denial and terror and the need to trust another person, to give oneself over to another's care.

A man tells me about his encounter with mycoplasma pneumonia, how he walked around for days with a cough and shaking chills, not willing to admit to himself that he was really ill. He felt relieved when a supervisor ordered him into the hospital. He describes then the embarrassment of waiting, undressed in a johnny to be admitted, all his control over his privacy suddenly taken away.

These people are physicians, but they were quite sobered by their experiences on the other side of the medical system.

Their reactions included phrases like "It's different when you're the patient."

"I hope I remember what it's like."

And "Every doctor should have to go through it."

They too as physicians remembered reactions that were not empathically congruent with their patient experience.

It is uncomfortable to feel what the patient is feeling. This is one of the reasons we tend to forget our own illness experiences. We protect ourselves from the feelings of fear and helplessness with anger, trying to deny that what is happening to them could be happening to us. To a certain extent we need to in order to do our jobs.

As a beginning medical student, I had difficulty drawing blood because of my concern about hurting the patients. In order to learn, it was necessary to approach venipuncture as a mechanical procedure. Unless I put aside the knowledge that it was another human being's arm, sensitive like mine, that I was jabbing, I was paralyzed. Then, for a long time, I was angry at any patient who was frightened or uncooperative. Eventually, I could empathize with the patient as well as do my job. I could acknowledge that it would hurt a little, give the patient a chance to prepare, to tell me when he or she was ready. My confidence then enabled me to tune everything out while I drew blood. But in other tasks I got impatient and frustrated still and was more distant from the patient.

Medicine becomes more efficient with each year, yet many patients feel lost in an impersonal system. This is not because of lack of physical contact, but lack of human contact. If we as physicians could keep our personal experiences as patients accessible, perhaps we could honestly say, when it is most needed, "I have an idea what you are going through and I'm willing to hear about it. I know you are frightened, but I want you to know I am here and will try to help you." I know how hard it is sometimes to think about the patient's experiences, but I also know that as a patient, it is what I want from my doctor.

---

om 'AN EXPERIENCE OF ILLNESS' to 'MY FATAL DISEASE'

Dr Armentano discovered the wall that existed between life as a physician and life as a patient. As a patient, she could be frightened and tormented, feel helpless and humiliated. By repressing those emotions, she was able to protect herself. Her defenses were so effective that they partly insulated her from the plight of the patient.

Despite its unpleasantness, Dr Armentano grasped the emotional implication of her abdominal pain and used it to gain understanding of how she functioned as a person and as a physician. Autognostic effort led her to recognize that those insulating defenses impaired her empathy. Valuing her capacity for empathy motivated her to confront her vulnerability.

The fear and pain that she shares with her patients recalled some of the effort that she had exerted to overcome the excessive empathy that had interfered with her function as a medical student. As with most physicians, her training and early medical experience leaned too far toward subduing her tendency to share the feelings of her patients.

Her episode of abdominal pain led Dr Armentano to cut a window in the wall between herself as a physician and herself as a patient. This enabled her to observe and to reach out to her patients in a healing and compassionate way without impairing her functioning as a physician. Like Dr Andrews, she encourages other physicians to make more contact with emotional reactions.

The same recommendation can be offered to nonphysicians who erect internal barriers. They become alienated from their fellows in guarding themselves against suffering.

The theme of illness in the physician is continued in the essay, "My Fatal Disease," by Dr Theo C. Manschreck. He observed the onset, intensification, and eventual decline of symptoms in himself.

Chapter 16

MY FATAL DISEASE

Theo C. Manschreck, M.D.

One cold Saturday I was skiing in northern New Hampshire, thoroughly enjoying myself. In the late afternoon, taking my time on a gentle hill, I was suddenly struck down by a hot dog skier whose reckless speed and careless disregard for the less skilled made collision inevitable. I went down in the snow, stunned but alert and angry. There was no pain or reduced mobility, and I got myself up, brushed off the snow, and continued skiing. I soon dismissed it. Not until much later did this little episode, so quickly forgotten, become part of a larger experience of anxiety and death.

That evening at the lodge I found a note to call my sister as soon as possible. I found that my grandmother had just died — suddenly, although not unexpectedly — at age 88.

My maternal grandmother was my only living grandparent. She had been in failing health for several years. An independent woman, she had left a small town in Kansas to live and to work in Washington, D.C., prior to World War II. I was her first grandson. Throughout my childhood, she had been close to me. Even when she lived in a different city, I saw her regularly. During first grade, I lived in Washington and this increased our contact. She was a proud and loving person, and it had been sad to see her grow more deaf, forgetful, and weak. Her death was my first close experience with death.

She had lived with my family after she retired. As she became old and feeble after the grandchildren left home, my parents were unable to care for her. Eventually we had to find her a rest home, run by her church.

The phone call could have been other bad news. My mother was in the midst of a workup of a breast lump, and I knew that a biopsy was pending. (As it turned out, the biopsy had been done the day before with preliminary negative pathology reports, but the official results were still not available.)

The rest of the evening and the next day I was consumed by sorrowful memories of grandmother and worry about mother. I began to trek back to Boston en route to Kansas, where Grandma was to be buried. Gradually, I became aware that I did not feel well. I felt physically sick. My sleep — normally unproblematic — became troublesome and insomnia set in. I became preoccupied with the fear of death. Persistent abdominal distress, with dull, throbbing, right upper quadrant pain distracted and frightened me. My strong history on both sides of the family for gall bladder and other gastrointestinal ailments came to mind and kept me awake.

As I started my flight to Kansas, I began to notice two changes, one an increasing pain in the right thigh radiating into the groin. Initially, I did not think much about this new pain; my thoughts were too sad. The second was a persistent uneasiness about flying, a surprise because I had never had it once during my years of air travel. I arrived in cold damp Wichita, Kansas, met the rest of the family, and began the unhappy preparations for the funeral.

The next two days were miserable. The penetrating cold was a constant distraction. During the preparations for burying the dead, I was able to ignore my own health worries. Yet when not involved in any specific activity, I found myself apprehensive about the variety of pains I was experiencing, particularly the groin pain. Anxiety grew. I grasped the possibility that I had contracted a fatal disease.

Having completed the unpleasant, but in some ways positive and constructive, rituals of saying good-bye to Grandma, I made my way home. Health concerns grew more intense, yet I did not share them with anyone. It was not easy to do, and I was hoping for a sudden remission. The flight east, routine for me, was marked by apprehension of an unclear sort; I kept looking out the window, couldn't read, noticed every change in engine sounds. I was afraid.

In Boston the next day, I secretly arranged to see a urologist. I needed to face the symptoms, one way or another. I could not go on the way I was feeling. The urologist was pleasant and matter-of-fact. He took a detailed history and listened to my prepared comments, edited for signs of malignant anxiety and omitting the overwhelming events of the previous week. His physical examination revealed no abnormal findings. Following further discussion and reassurance, I was told, "Okay, there is really no problem." The diagnosis was a pulled muscle in the groin, "probably related to unusual exertion."

There was no evidence of tumor! The "cancer" had originated in my snowy collision. I made the appropriate additional diagnoses.

Somatic symptoms continued on and off for two months after Grandma's death, then began to resolve. There was, however, a complication. The persistent uneasiness of my flight to Kansas turned out to be the first episode of two years of fear of flying. I started ruminating about airplane crashes, especially whenever it was necessary to fly. Associations to caskets, traps, and loss of control haunted me whenever I stepped into an airplane. The fear increased for several days before a flight. My office window, coincidentally facing a main flight path of planes leaving Logan Airport, became a constant symbol of death.

Though I knew why I was suffering this way and that with time, things would be better, the knowledge did not penetrate to the symptoms themselves.

Only with time, I gradually returned to normal.

From 'MY FATAL DISEASE' to 'A WRITING BLOCK'

In the events before and after his grandmother's death, Dr Manschreck did not confide in anyone about his physical ailment, although he spent a lot of time talking about his grief. He attempted to cope with the pain and fear alone, using reason as his instrument.

He was aware that his fear, insomnia, and pain in his groin related to his bereavement. As an experienced psychiatrist, Dr Manschreck certainly knew that talking about an experience of grief is one of the most effective ways of overcoming its painful aftermath.

In our hospital, he is held in warm regard. He must have known that many of his colleagues and former teachers would have been sympathetic and accepting had he spoken to us about what he was going through.

Yet with all his professional and personal resources, it seems likely that Dr Manschreck did not shorten the period of his distress. Did he cling to those symptoms to prevent the reality of her death from reaching him emotionally? Her death, as he wrote, was too sudden. He allowed his recognition of her death, deep down, to occur gradually over a two-year period by retaining his symptoms. Did this allow her to depart from his inner life slowly?

People who suffer even uncomplicated bereavement tend to experience symptoms such as insomnia, appetite change, or other physical symptoms for about six months to two years. This seems to be a natural process. It appears to be a way that people allow the actuality of the death of someone dear or important to sink in slowly. Others experience complicated grief reactions that sometimes go on for many years. The complication in Dr Manschreck's grief reaction was his fear of flying. It lasted for two years, and maybe that is the amount of time that he needed to deal with her loss.

We have learned from psychoanalysis and psychotherapy that part of the process of grieving involves giving up a relationship as it had been experienced over time. The adult had to give up his grandmother, but so did the young man, the adolescent, and especially the little boy, the first grandson.

Had he experienced fears, like the ones he described about flying, when he was a little boy? Had his grandmother comforted him? Would she have been able to make those fears disappear? Were his fears of flying a way of crying out to her, to maintain the illusion that she was not gone? The theme of death of someone close to the psychiatrist continues in the next essay. In "A Writing Block," Dr Sidney Zisook reveals to us other effects of the death of someone important.

Chapter 17

A WRITING BLOCK

Sidney Zisook, M.D.

A few years ago I was asked to write a chapter on "Psychological Aspects of Urological Cancer." I gladly accepted. I had been teaching the human sexuality course to residents and medical students at the University of Texas and had strong academic interests in psychological aspects of medical illness. I assumed this would be an easy task.

My normal modus operandi for writing is to mull things over for a few days, review the literature for a week or two, and then sit down and write a first draft over the course of several hours. This paper was different. My "mulling-over" period was greatly expanded and not as well focused or directed as usual. After weeks of thinking, I wasn't sure what I wanted to say or how to say it. I felt it was best to get onto the second stage, reviewing the literature, which might stimulate some sense of direction.

Reviewing the literature was uniquely different. I spent hours upon hours in the library abstracting articles that were only peripherally related to the subject. For some reason I was not dealing with urological cancer at all but stockpiling articles on psychological aspects of illness or cancer, avoiding those pertaining to the urogenital system. I thought I needed to get a general idea of how I wanted to direct the paper before specifically dealing with the subject at hand. I found myself gathering an ever-growing collection of reprints only tangentially related to urological cancer.

Despite my rationalizations, I was finally able to obtain and abstract articles specifically related to psychological aspects of urogenital cancer. The next stage, sitting down and writing, was even more difficult. Once I sit down with three or four sharpened pencils and a pad of yellow legal paper I am able to write a first draft without difficulty, but this time, I couldn't even get out a first sentence. It was painful and frustrating. Evening after evening I would sit down at my desk and end up with nothing but a wastebasket full of crumpled yellow paper. I started to ask myself why I was having such difficulty, but I wasn't able to come up with any answers. Then, when taking a break, I challenged my son to a board game of "hockey." I wasn't sure why I thought of playing this game. It had been lying under my bed gathering dust for years. He reluctantly accepted the challenge and we played; and I in turn, rather uncharacteristically, beat him soundly rather than letting him stay close or beat me. After our game I sat down with my wife to discuss the problems I was having with this paper.

We talked and eventually my wife asked whether the problem was related to my cousin's death. He died of testicular cancer during my early adolescence. We had been best friends, inseparable in our childhood. Several associations relating my son, the hockey game, my cousin, and the paper flooded me. First of all, my son was named for my cousin. The hockey game that I had just so soundly trounced him in was one I had bought years earlier while shopping for Christmas presents. Buying something for myself was totally out of character, but it looked like fun and I did it on impulse. But no one would play the game with me, and soon it gathered dust in its place under my bed. The last time I saw my cousin alive was during a Christmas vacation, shortly before he died. I visited him during the vacation while he was at the Mayo Clinic and searching for a miracle. The last night we were together, just before Christmas, we went to a hockey game. He wasn't feeling well but forced himself to go, to be a good host. I went home the next day; he died soon afterward, and I never saw him again.

My wife went to put my son to bed, and I then sat alone and thought about my cousin for the first time in years. I wondered whether I had guilt over that hockey game or whether I was angry at him for leaving so abruptly. I began to cry. Over the next few hours I re-experienced both painful and joyous memories of our childhood together.

The next morning I sat down at my desk, took up my pencil, and wrote the paper in a single draft.

From 'A WRITING BLOCK' to 'THE MISSING ITEMS'

It appears from "A Writing Block" that one of the greatest resources in expanding one's useful inner knowledge is to have a sensitive, responsive, and perceptive spouse. Dr Zisook contributed to the effectiveness of his wife's wise observation. In the first place, he sought her counsel in discussing his predicament about the paper he was trying to write. Second, he paid attention to her question about his cousin. Third, he allowed his associations and eventually his emotions to well up and emerge.

The experience illustrates how memories can be hidden for years, steeped in intense emotion. It shows the intricate network of feelings, memories, symbols, and inhibitions that repressed grief can produce. It also shows how unblocking those repressed emotions releases both the tears and the skills.

In "The Missing Items," Dr Alexander L. Miller illustrates the importance of paying serious attention to what is said by patients, just as Dr Zisook was led to insight by attending to an inspired observation by his wife.

Chapter 18

THE MISSING ITEMS

Alexander L. Miller, M.D.

When she came into the room she handed me a piece of paper, a copy of a page in a journal. This was not unusual; she often brought in items for me that she thought conveyed a message or might interest me.

"I thought of you when I read number 570."

I scanned the title ("A Factor Analysis of Missing Items from the MMPI") and on down the page.

570. "I find it difficult to think of anything to say when confronted with a room full of ducks."

"I thought of you at the end of a day of seeing patients when I read that."

I looked at some of the other items. 569. "Brussels sprouts make me sad." 574. "I sometimes think there are wild orgies all around me and I wonder why I am never invited." 580. "I am disgusted or frightened by blimps." Why 570? I thought.

"You must find it frustrating to have to deal with people like me all the time."

"What do you mean?"

"Oh, people with silly problems who don't feel like talking about them when they see you."

This was a familiar theme, asking to be enticed into talking and to be reassured that I valued what she said, but more was going on. Why the stuff on the room full of ducks? The session wore on and more emerged about the question of whether I really cared, or was I just interested in my research. Aha! Ducks, animals, rats — she knew my research involved working with animals, that was the connection. But no, there was more than that. It was, as they — we — say, an overdetermined statement. There was the sense of someone being confronted by a strange situation, the sense of being out of place. What was I doing in a room full of ducks?

The referral had come from medicine — please treat this lady's depression, she has all the vegetative signs and symptoms. But after a few meetings, it was abundantly clear that under the vegetation were longstanding maladaptive behavior patterns, major unresolved conflicts from an early age, and an ambivalent wish for insight and change. We discussed insight-oriented psychotherapy and agreed to meet weekly. We had been meeting for about two months. This was the first person I had seen in psychotherapy since leaving Boston. My thoughts drifted back.

A couple of years before leaving Boston I had gone up to my old prep school to play in the alumni hockey game. I was in good physical shape from jogging. I had only skated a couple of times in the dozen years since college, but I knew it would be like riding a bicycle.

Ho, ho! Not only could those kids skate like whirlwinds and check like linebackers, but the rules had been changed. The former sanctity of the defensive zone was gone. Forwards could now crash into defensemen where before only defensemen could crash into forwards. As a defenseman, I was most affronted by this intrusion into my space. Late in the game the indignity of it all came to a head when some teenage behemoth pinned me up against the boards, and his skate knocked my skate blade loose from its bracket. I wobbled off the ice in disarray.

After the game there was beer for the alumni. My wife smiled sympathetically at me when I came out of the dressing room. We got our beers and looked around. There were few familiar faces. Most were younger, recent graduates. A few were older. The conversations swirled around us. What are you majoring in, where do you want to go to medical school, what club do you play with, where do you practice, did you know so-and-so is playing goalie for the what's-their-names now? It was hard to know where to join in. I didn't feel like I was part of what was going on, like I was confronted with a room full of ducks.

It didn't take a lot of soul-searching to respond to the next alumni hockey game invitation.

It wasn't important to me that I got back to being a hockey player. Perhaps I couldn't be good again. Who cared? I had had some good years. I had had the team camaraderie and a bit of glory. The memories and fruits of that experience were intact, didn't need reinforcement. I was comfortable with Miller the ex-hockey player. How about Miller the ex-therapist?

I chose my psychiatry residency with the specific intention of getting both research experience and training in psychodynamic psychotherapy. Faculty and fellow residents attached great importance to the experience of doing and receiving psychotherapy, to interpreting the transference, and so on. I met with my patients, I discussed them formally and informally, I learned the lingo, I learned to identify the underlying issues. I developed some skills I hadn't had and some pride in how I used them. For four years after residency I continued to see a small number of psychotherapy patients, though most of my patient-care time was spent doing a combination of pharmacotherapy and supportive therapy. Then I moved.

Months went by before I saw my first psychotherapy referral. He came once. Then I began seeing the depressed woman. It would be like riding a bicycle again. Ho, ho! In truth, it was like confronting a room full of ducks. It had been months since I had terminated with my psychotherapy patients, but years since I had started with them. My timing was off; my third ear heard "quack, quack"; I floundered. Or maybe I wasn't so bad, but just thought so. It didn't matter, I had come to terms with what was happening.

There was more soul-searching than after the alumni hockey game, but the answer was the same — no more. I didn't want to put in the time and effort to become good again. I referred the patient to one of the faculty actively involved in doing psychotherapy.

What's the point? Where's the moral? Can you put it all together? Yes. Joe Schwartz was right when he told us residents that it's a mistake to see too few psychotherapy patients because each one assumes too much importance. I didn't want to see more, so I had to see none. Yes. It means that there is a set of skills that need constant sharpening, that grow rusty with disuse, and without which we feel awkward and out of place.

Was it a waste then, this specialized training and experience? Was it just bodybuilding, only to let it all go to flab? No, not at all. It was a lastingly rewarding experience. Well, then, was it like the hockey—a pleasant time in Denver on the way to San Francisco, a girlfriend you loved but didn't marry? Yes, there's some of that, but something else happened over time. The ways of thinking, conceptualizing, being aware, got translated into a new language, a new set of skills more appropriate to a different set of clinical circumstances and to my particular style. I was never really comfortable with the form of formal psychotherapy, and the less I did, the more this discomfort showed. Then, one day, a patient came in and told me to quack or get off the pond. Which I did.

From 'THE MISSING ITEMS' to 'PATIENTS AND CHILDREN'

Dr Miller illustrated for us some of the qualities of psychotherapeutic listening. He heard what the patient said and tried to understand it. He was not satisfied by a single fragment of meaning that he discovered: the connection with his animal research. Applying the principle of multiple determination, he sought additional signficance to the patient's comment.

He avoided a common pitfall of automatically ascribing negative comments about the therapist to transference. The latter refers to the attribution to the therapist of qualities, feelings, attitudes, or ideas that the patient had experienced previously with a significant person in his life. It is tempting to ascribe unfavorable remarks to transference and to accept praise at face value. The skillful and competent psychotherapist will apply objectivity, skepticism, and curiosity to both kinds of comments.

As Dr Miller followed his inquiry, he allowed himself to notice associations and memories as they led back to his experience in the hockey game and to features of his training in psychiatry. As one of his former teachers, I can vouch for his talent as a potential psychotherapist. I never saw him play hockey. If his abilities in hockey had been comparable to his talent for the conduct of psychotherapy, he might have had a career in the pros.

He was able to give up both activities. He showed us how he was able to retain the best of his experience as a hockey player and as a psychotherapist, and he was able to relinquish the rest. This is one of the ways that a healthy individual can maintain conditions of comfort and satisfaction inwardly. One does not need to have exceptional talent. A person's experience can be examined in such a way as to extract and retain that which is most valuable. The rest can be recognized, experienced emotionally, evaluated, and let go.

The theme of the death of someone close to the doctor returns in the next essay. The psychiatrist, Dr Rege Stewart, tells us how she tried to prevent her personal bereavement from interfering with her professional duty.

Chapter 19

PATIENTS AND CHILDREN

Rege Stewart, M.D.

Self understanding is a lifetime process that continues after training is finished; neither cognitive knowledge nor psychiatric insight stops developing after the training period. One should also be able to interpret the psychodynamics of everyday interactions and eventually modify one's own behavior to become more effective.

How does autognosis work? Let me try to illustrate it through some personal experiences.

My husband and I had planned on a large family when we married. I was going to have a part-time career to accommodate raising four or five children. Unfortunately, our dream never materialized. Because of various medical complications, I had experienced multiple miscarriages. Added to this was the problem that I was RH-negative and my husband was RH-positive. Our first child had problems with blood incompatibility. My fifth pregnancy was especially stressful because it occurred during my psychiatry training and also because I had to undergo amniocentesis every two weeks. Computerized tomographic scans were not available yet and amniocentesis had to be done blindly. This presented a constant worry about the welfare of the fetus and concern about iatrogenic complications.

My pregnancy was made more difficult by the fact that two of my severely impaired patients had difficulty dealing with my condition. Particularly, one of the patients expressed intense hostility toward me for daring to get pregnant and not devoting all my time to her care. She expressed jealousy about the baby and felt that by having it, I would take time away from her treatment. She also had expressed the wish and the hope that the baby would die. Another patient predicted that my baby was going to die because he had a bad spell on him and everybody he came in contact with died. Of course, these statements reflected the patients' own conflicts and feelings about themselves. As a therapist, I carefully explored the reason for these projections. In the case of the first patient, my pregnancy reactivated repressed sibling rivalry, while in the second patient, it reflected the patient's omnipotent and nihilistic delusional symptom from depression.

Nevertheless, these projective fantasies complicated my grief when the baby died. Just prior to delivery, she died from umbilical cord compression.

When I started seeing my patients, I had to make a decision whether to tell them the truth or to pretend that everything was fine. As a grieving mother, it would have been easier for me to share my experience and gain support. Yet, as a therapist, I realized that this reality would overwhelm my two patients who were so angry about my pregnancy. It would confirm their fantasy of omnipotence and destructiveness and would result in tremendous guilt. This certainly would have complicated their therapy and conceivably could have led to their decompensation. Thus, I decided to portray an outward appearance that everything was fine.

If a patient asked about the baby, why didn't I just throw back the question and examine the motive for it? After all, this is an acceptable method to deal with personal questions in psychotherapy. Frankly, I did not go into detailed exploration, because I was hurting too much. I could pretend serenity and happiness for a few fleeting minutes, but I was afraid that the facade would shatter under stress. I just did not have the emotional strength to maintain the deception under hostile projection.

Most of my patients would have handled the news graciously and even supportively, but for the sake of the few who could not, I had to make this decision.

I always assumed that in the face of a real tragedy I would succumb to depression. I was surprised to find that instead of depression, I felt intense anger. Anger at God for allowing my daughter to die senselessly, and anger at and jealousy of other pregnant women who could have the joy of a healthy baby. Both the intensity and the very presence of the anger surprised me. Why wasn't I feeling sad or depressed? While reflecting on this, I realized how acceptable it would be for me to give in to feelings of depression and self-pity. Partially, I made a conscious decision not to allow myself the luxury of grieving. I wanted to shelter my 4-year-old son from the painful reality. As a psychiatrist, I knew how anxiety- and guilt-inducing a sibling's death can be for a preschool child. I also was aware how children at this age magically assume guilt for the depression of their parents. I couldn't burden my son with this. Although I had no control over my daughter's death, I certainly had control over how I reacted to it: I was going to go on as if nothing happened and grieve silently and privately. Only my husband and a few colleagues and friends knew how desperate I felt.

My husband and I decided against a funeral. The baby was buried in an unmarked grave by the funeral home. My denial was both conscious and unconscious. When I was reviewing the checks a month later, I found one written out for a funeral home. My immediate thought was that one of the relatives must have died and we paid for part of the funeral. It took me several minutes to realize that it was for our daughter.

Why was I so angry? Why was I angry at God? For months, I couldn't enter church without the tears rolling down my cheeks. I puzzled over that question for weeks. Gradually, through a lot of self-reflection, I came to understand. I was raised in a religious home and I felt that God always rewards "good" behavior. I had the fantasy that if I was reasonably good, God would reward me with a life full of blessings. As long as I was on God's side, life would give me everything I desired. I was good so how could God do this to me? I was angry because I felt betrayed by God. Did God really exist? Did He care how I felt? Did He care that I was angry with Him?

Gradually, it dawned on me that my thinking represented an omnipotent fantasy and a childhood wish to be always the favorite daughter. Growing up I was the favorite daughter in my family and was always treated preferentially. I hoped life would treat me preferentially too. Does this mean that God does not exist? Not really. I still believe in God, but my understanding is less magical and self-serving.

It took about six months before I could talk about the death of my daughter without bursting into tears. I never thought that I would ever come to peace with her death or the likelihood of not having another child. Healing came with the arrival of our adopted daughter five years later.

We decided to name our adopted daughter Sharon rather than Sarah, a name I set aside for our biological daughter. I was concerned whether I could bond as well as I did to our biological son. When she cried the first night at home (she was 4 days old), I rushed into the nursery, hugged her, and said, "It is okay, Sarah." It took me a few seconds to realize that my Freudian slip indicated that, on an unconscious level, I had accepted Sharon already as my own. An awareness of my unconscious feelings signaled not only bonding, but also healing.

From 'PATIENTS AND CHILDREN' to 'CULTURE AS AUTOGNOSIS'

Dr Stewart deliberately exercised powerful self-control to protect her patients and her son. She predicted that the impact on her patients and on her son of the death of her infant would have been too intense.

It was not merely a way for her to avoid her feelings. As she revealed to us, she was intensely aware of sadness and anger. She cried to herself and revealed her distress to her husband and to a few friends and colleagues.

The intensity of her loss is easy to imagine. My own reaction on first reading the essay was one of shock, numbness, distress, and sadness. I had not known that she had lost her daughter. My personal regard for Dr Stewart accounted for some of the intensity of my own reaction. It is hard to imagine any sentient person reading this essay who would not be moved by the experience to some extent. A vulnerable 4-year-old son and severely impaired hate-filled patients might have been overwhelmingly affected.

Even now, after many readings, it is difficult for me to comment as an editor who has a responsibility to underscore the significance of what the essay reveals. My personal inclination is to embrace my former student, whom I have not seen for many years, and perhaps to cry with her. That may never actually happen. It might remain a fantasy.

Following her example, perhaps I can focus on a particular lesson that this essay can provide for many people. Dr Stewart used the phrase, "the luxury of grieving," and she decided not to allow herself that luxury.

She meant that she would not allow herself to express feelings spontaneously whenever they arose. She decided that she would exercise control over how she reacted. This does not mean that she failed to grieve. She decided that she would guide her grief.

The luxury of grief is available to many people, but certainly not to all. There are many who have responsibilities, people to protect. One of the great accomplishments described in this essay is that Dr Stewart was able to grieve in a healthy way, to allow her feelings to come forth in situations in which they would do no harm. She did this sufficiently to allow herself to recover and to grow as a person. She showed us that channeling the grieving process can still lead to further personal development and to healing.

Dr Stewart's essay revealed experiences focused on the family. She examined her individual experience and explored it deeply. Yet the events that evoked her feelings were connected with her baby, her son, her family, and the family from which she came.

The next essay, by Dr Arthur Kleinman, focuses on the family imbedded in a wider culture. Dr Stewart's experience is painful and familiar in its recognition of individuality. Dr Kleinman's essay tells us about what is unfamiliar to most of us and had been unfamiliar long ago to him.

Chapter 20

CULTURE AS AUTOGNOSIS:
An Outer Journey toward the Self

Arthur Kleinman, M.D.

In D.M. Thomas' surprisingly popular (because pornographic) yet deeply serious (because moral) novel, *The White Hotel*, there sleeps a mighty dragon. It contains a cultural critique of the psychoanalytic perspective that I took to be clinically compelling, but that most psychiatric clinicians seem to have found entirely avoidable: To wake up the beast might create more havoc than Massons' overblown antics. That cultural critique of psychoanalysis, which in less elegant if more methodologically rigorous form has been advanced off and on principally by anthropologists and, surprisingly less often and less successfully, by cross-cultural psychiatrists, is part of the "wisdom" of the cultural perspective. Like most "wisdom" in academia today, it tends to get buried under the statistical tests, tables of numerical data, abstruse theoretical constructs, minutiae of ethnographic detail, and the sheer boredom that academic prose seems to be intended to create. The point, however, is simple and direct: Thomas' fictionalized Freud fails (and indeed must fail) in his treatment of Thomas' equally fictitious case because he leaves out of the analysis of transference and countertransference the perilous cultural fact (to which both are blind because they are unable to step ouside their cultural ethos), that the treatment is undertaken by Jewish patient and Jewish analyst in German society in the early

101

1930s at the very moment when that society is being expropriated by the Nazis and the Jews are being readied for genocide. The heroine, after her "analysis," ends up in the death machinery of the Holocaust possessing (would that this were her only defeat) an incomplete psychological understanding of herself and others that is gruesomely perfected by a dawning sociological insight into the horror of a culture gone amok not from insanity but from evil. The hermeneutics of suspiciousness, Thomas seems to want us to understand, cannot be applied to man's inner life until it has helped him interpret his place in a particular world; indeed the two, culture and consciousness, are systematically related.

This abstract point is the gist of the anthropological vision, the essence of cross-cultural experience. It also represents what is valid in my own personal autognostic encounter with myself, not the difficult product of an interior journey on the analyst's couch, but the no less hard-won insight of an outer quest in a non-Western culture (Chinese society) where I have lived and conducted field research for more than 4 of the last 20 years. This journey liberated me, professionally and personally, from the ethnocentrism and psychocentrism that are the Scylla and Charybdis of the century-old movement of modernism that has come to dominate and distort the Western sense of self as much as it has created the other alienating self-images of our age. How did it (not the oppressive introspection of modernism but the self-liberation through cultural encounter) come about?

THE SOCIOCENTRIC SELF

PERSONAL EXPERIENCE VIEWED THROUGH A CHINESE LOOKING GLASS

It is summer 1969 in downtown Taipei, Taiwan. Two Americans are meeting for lunch. One is a surgeon in the United States Public Health Service detached from the National Institutes of Health to do research at the local United States Naval Medical Research Unit and 4 months into a 14-month tour of duty. He will later author this paper, though if you could tell him at the time that still ahead will be training in psychiatry and anthropology, he would not unlikely think you were quite mad. The other is a seasoned anthropologist, veteran of many field trips to Taiwan over almost a decade and a half and now considered by the members of "his" village virtually an honorable elder. We shall refer to this senior China scholar as Professor B.G. At one point in the course of their spicy Sichuanese lunch, perhaps stimulated by all the hot peppers, the young man turns to the, then new, friend, initiating something like the following conversation:

Kleinman: "You know, I've been here only a few months but I can't help being struck by the basic similarities underlying all the surface differences between Chinese and Americans."

Professor B.G.: "That's interesting, Arthur. You see I've been here all these years off and on, living in the village and in Taipei, travelling all around, making all sorts of Chinese friends, reading widely, and me, I'm impressed with the differences! Even at a deep level."

Something rare and, in retrospect, profound happened to me at that moment. It wasn't simply the embarrassment of the neophyte being contradicted by the expert, though I remember feeling a bit foolish for just that reason at the time. It was much more like the sudden heuristic shock that gives insight into the extent of one's own ignorance, which since Socrates' maieutic pedagogy, we in the West have come to take as the beginning of self-knowledge. This is what Buddhists regard as the first step on the ladder of transcendence: recognizing the reality of one's desperate existential situation in the world. I knew in an instant not only that I might be (and probably was) wrong in my facile appeal to the psychic unity of mankind, which was grounded in very limited experience, but that I could be very wrong indeed. If I was mistaken, I might be mystifying myself, falsifying my experience, confusing the peripheral for the central, at a fundamental level getting it all wrong.

This possibility was more than just of passing concern to me. It held a vital personal meaning. Overtly, I felt a threat to my shaky orientation to the bewildering sounds, smells, noises, the sheer busyness and vibrancy of the Chinese reality that pressed in upon me, asserting its (in my view) differences as (in their view) common sense, the way things are. The possibility that these differences were not merely surface phenomena but substantial divergences in human experience attacked my professional (and quite American) conviction in the determinative powers of the objective world of biology (I was running a small clinical immunology laboratory at the time), the universal scientific bedrock beneath the sedimentary layers of epiphenomenal psychological and cultural reality that is still the practical epistemology of the biomedical model. Through a long search, I had come to place my faith (again quite American) in equity, justice, the innate equality of individuals regardless of ethnic or class background, even my abhorrence of American involvement in the Vietnam War, which was then raging, on what I now began to perceive was a very slippery slope indeed.

I remember sitting back in my chair, putting my chopsticks down, and starting to think hard. For my anthropologist friend had said the one thing I knew I feared coming to terms with: that we are not alike at the core, that differences in language and behavior cannot be explained away, that I had misled myself to believe I could arrive at an understanding of Chinese culture intuitively: out of goodwill, empathy, a fervent belief in equality and pragmatism, and a fear of being turned back by linguistic and cultural barriers that were enormous but that I had the need to vault nonetheless.

Two aspects of my personal history need to be understood to make sense of my shaken reaction to Professor B.G.'s seemingly innocuous riposte. The first piece of biography, sad to tell, is that as a child in an alarmingly dangerous Bedford section of Brooklyn, I had become by 11 years of age something of an inchoate delinquent who commanded a ragamuffin gang of brats, not much by present standards but bullies all the same, predatory enough to know how to get by in an ethnically polyglot community where intimidation by brute force and the wily ways of the survivor held cachet. One day my foul-mouthed crowd surrounded an 11-year-old Chinese girl and her two small brothers who were the scions of the family who ran the neighborhood Chinese laundry. This girl was in my class at P.S. 161, and when my gang began shouting racial slurs at her, she broke through the circle of tormentors and with tears streaming down her face and a brother holding tightly to each arm, she shouted at me as I stood grinning at the nasty goings on: "Why do you torment us? What have we done to you? Do you hate us because we are Chinese?" Like Stonewall Jackson in John Greenleaf Whittier's wretched poem, "Barbara Fritchie," which our homeroom teacher was forcing us to memorize, "a shade of sadness, a blush of shame over the face of the leader came." Dishonored, and properly so, I turned away and angrily called off my pack of pediatric cronies ("who touches a hair on yon grey head, dies like a dog, March on; he said.") I took the moral lesson thoroughly to heart (though I had been ready to do so for some time), thank God, and slunk off to exchange a better and brighter future for street-wise bigotry. I think from that point onward I both swallowed the melting pot ideology hook, line, and sinker, and as an assimilated, detribalized, secular American ethnic, I adopted the psychic unity of mankind as a fundamental tenet.

The second piece of biography comes from a trip I made to Europe in the summer of 1962. During that semester Wanderjahr, I spent some marvelously peaceful weeks in Germany, living in Heidelberg and Berlin, hiking the ordered paths of the Odenwald, making all sorts of friends along the way, and improving my German language skills. A Jew in the land of my people's genocide, I spent hardly any time, as far as I can remember, thinking about the horrors of 17 years before. Such is the self-deceit of adolescence, I never pressed my hosts about their activities under Hitler. But when I reached the Rhine, I experienced an awful epiphany, a slowly dawning recognition that speaks to me still of the need to interpret beneath the surface of things. I was strolling in the outskirts of a small town on the French side of the Rhine, walking along a canal when it began to rain hard. To avoid the sudden summer storm, I raced toward a distant copse of willows. So hard did I run that as I passed between the trees I had to hold up my hands to soften the impact of pushing open a thin metal gate and bounding against a large smooth object. I recall turning my head sideways and noticing a star of David, then turning back to look at the marble pillar up against which I had lodged myself. It was a large, red tombstone. I had run into a small Jewish cemetery. I could read the family name on the tombstone: Rubin. There were I believe 11 personal names. You could tell by the dates of birth who were the grandparents, their children, their grandchildren. The date of death of each was the same day. That seemed strange. I was confused, then became uneasy. A terrible understanding was working its way through the romance of summer out into the harsher light of history. At first, incredible as it later seemed, I denied the half-formulated insight. There must have been some catastrophe: an accident, flood, some other horrible "natural" disaster. I hurried back to my pension and inquired of the very proper, middle-aged proprietress (who must have been as old then as I am now) what had happened on such and such a day, the date the last three generations of the Rubin family had ceased to exist. She stuttered, hesitated, became embarrassed, and kept repeating, "The war. You know. The war." My very limited French fell apart as fast as did her English, and without recognizing the fateful irony we switched to German. The words came out fast, hot, bloody. I felt I would vomit, so physical had the sensation of horror become. I asked questions, but things went from bad to worse. I had the distinct feeling that there was something further she couldn't say, or wouldn't. My suspicions grew and I fantasized that we were now standing in the Rubins' house, which she and her family had acquired after the SS had lined the 11 Rubins up by the canal and murdered them. But I never did find out the reason why she withheld from me the full story: Maybe it was better than the evil I conjured up, or perhaps worse.

It took little time for me to master a lesson Jews and other despised ethnic groups have learned repeatedly. Things are not what they seem. The construction of reality is different from how it is popularly portrayed, and the difference can be a matter of life or death.

Paradoxically, since that time, I have been partial not to detective stories that discern the light of truth through the fog of deceit (which one might take to be the message at the end of the tale), but to the story of the three baseball umpires and judgments about defining social reality (which one might take as the message of the first part of the experience).

"Some is balls and some is strikes, I calls them as they is," says the first.

"Some is balls and some's strikes, I call them as I see them," responds the second.

"Some is balls and some is strikes, but they ain't nothing until I calls them," states the third, who obviously knows something about life and the social construction of reality.

These echos from the past came to me as I looked across the half-eaten dishes of the Chinese luncheon to where Professor B.G. was sitting, looking at me in my silent consternation warmly bemused.

He was right. Dead right!

It is the gift of the anthropological approach to cross-cultural experience to disclose that counter to the tourist's intuition of sameness the world is thought and lived differently. The self, for example, is here conceived and valued as individual, independent, autonomous, directly confrontive, even heroic in a romantic sense, [1] while elsewhere (for example Chinese culture) it is understood and expected to be group, especially family, centered, dependent, concerned more with the harmonious balancing of social relations than assertion of the ego, indirect in coping styles, situationally oriented, highly pragmatic. [2] Behavior follows belief and norm. In Chinese culture, depression is rarely experienced as existential despair but as a somatic experience in which overt vegetative complaints covertly enter into negotiations in the family. Social relations, not intrapsychic experience, are the chief forms of concern. Guilt is uncommonly associated with depression in China or Taiwan. Female infants are still occasionally killed in rural areas of both societies, despite government laws, because in cultural terms they are not yet fully human and their existence matters less than family priorities.

I could pile case upon case, belief upon belief to demonstrate a cultural otherness that can be understood but that is a different experience of the life world, a different way of being. In Buddhist society, Sri Lanka for example, generalized hopelessness, which in the West we associate with negative conditions in the psychodynamics of depression, [3] is regarded positively as the first step on the ladder of Buddhist transcendence, a wisdom about the world publicly articulated in Buddhist values as fundamentally frustrating. The individual's task is to withdraw all cathexes from the world and self, indeed to efface the self. Hence, the bereaved and the elderly preparing for death in Sri Lanka voluntarily take upon themselves the practice of *sil*, meditation on revulsion (corpses, feces, etc.). [4] In many places in India touching (which we tend to regard as a universal emblem of love and caring) may be viewed with abhorrence as polluting if it crosses caste lines or if a menstruating Brahmin mother touches her son. [5] The Ilongot of the Philippines traditionally mastered grief by raiding neighbors and taking their heads, [6] which they threw to the ground feeling at the same time a lightening of the load of sadness. Geertz [7] describes a Javanese man carrying on a conversation shortly after his wife died that demonstrates his strongly culturally affirmed skill in soothing his emotions into a placid smoothness — not an act for the visitor but a lived experience. For much of the non-Western world the emptiness of loss is not just conceived but experienced as soul loss. [5] Many excellent studies demonstrate the extraordinary cultural variety of personal experience. [8-11]

What the anthropological experience teaches, and taught me, is that these differences are systematic not adventitious or random. They are part of a system, a local cultural system, linking conception of self, norms guiding social relations, folk beliefs about deviance and pathology, forms of etiquette, sociolinguistic codes for negotiating relations of relative power in family, work place, and community. The ethnographer interprets these systems by first removing himself from the cultural commonsensical world he was raised in, entering an alien society with distinctive beliefs and values, learning the language well enough to be able to speak with people at length and in detail about salient aspects of experience, living as the natives do and for a long enough period (one or two years) in a local community to participate in and observe daily life. This is a profoundly difficult and rewarding experience for most of us who have undergone its rigors. Cultural commonsense views of one proper way of doing things give way to recognition of a plurality of life ways and the social construction of self as much as religion, of kinship as thoroughly as legal system, of morality as well as economy.

In this movement outward toward another world, there is a complementary process of rethinking and recreating the self. We recognize and begin to discard biases; we begin chameleon-like to take on aspects of the culture we study—not just dress, style of movement, and conversation, but categories of thought. We try some on and discover they fit, others we shrink from and wonder what it would mean to our own sense of self to think them and live them. We become impressed with a phenomenon that Zen masters and Morita psychotherapists use. When we begin to change our external behavior in a systematic way supported by the culture around us, our inner experience begins to change. It is hard for you to grasp this if you have not done it or for me to convince you of its authenticity. But after you have learned how to efface and disguise the more egotistical aspects of self in a Chinese community, learned to communicate about one's self with subtle indirection, learned to maintain group cohesion and harmony as the chief objective—over months and years something in us changes. Of course we don't become Chinese, or even observe a radical shift in personality. Yet, nonetheless, we recreate ourselves differently in social encounters and when we are by ourselves.

In my own case, years of experience in Chinese culture have influenced not only dietary habits but my view of family, of psychiatric practice, and of self. I notice that I organized my clinical work in the United States, even with white patients, around the problem of somatization, perhaps the culturally most salient problem among Chinese patients. I think my wife, who is a sinologist, and I are extremely family centered. We both have backgrounds that emphasize family values so this is not a new direction for us, but compared with peers we have developed a heightened family orientation that cannot but have been supported by our involvement with a culture that holds this value-orientation as most central. As for self, I think I came to know myself better by seeing me through the reactions of Chinese friends, patients, and research subjects, and by experiencing daily life in a Chinese context. I have worn off at least some of the sharper edges of an assertive ego, become more comfortable with dependency needs, redefined ambition on behalf of family as well as self, become both a little less psychological and much more somatically introspective, and also more interested and skilled in interpersonal communication through subtlety and indirection. Running up against cultural differences has encouraged a kind of self-analysis that emphasizes empathy, the alternative viewpoint, and seeing the self as others see it, a sort of perspectivism, or cultural analysis of countertransference. I don't believe these abiding changes have been enormous, nor do they stem only from the cross-cultural experience. Certainly, other kinds of experiences might have fostered them had my life and career trajectories been different.

One change in self concept that has been fundamentally influenced by the Chinese experience has been concern for health maintenance, personal prevention, and mastery in illness experiences of anxiety and uncertainty. Again each of these coping orientations is strongly embedded in traditional Chinese culture and was the source of considerable self-learning in my years of studying illness and care in Chinese settings.

Through these experiences, I came to regard the self as much more malleable than we in psychiatry regard it to be. It is almost as if the self is reshaped and recreated in life experience in which the background of personality, family, and work provides continuity while changing situations, relationships, and meanings are templates for discontinuities. There is a dialectic between self and environment that a sociocentric culture like Chinese culture amplifies. At this point there has been so much feedback between the two poles of the dialectic between self and culture, I am not sure where one leaves off and the other begins.

The thrust of my argument, then, is that autognosis for me has taken the form of an outward journey through Chinese culture toward the self. Could I have gotten here by other routes? Probably! When I arrived would I have found the same self? I think not. I have often thought of conducting a study of the personal meaning of field experience for anthropologists. I would be a perfect subject for such a study.

Perhaps one other point is important. It has been my clinical impression that for middle-aged, middle-class men in American society, a key developmental task is coming to terms with one's mortality (and its early signs in the aging process) in a secular society that avoids the question of personal death, that glamourizes youth, and makes the aging process seem frightening, and that unlike traditional cultures offers no promise of immortality (symbolic or real) as a meaning with which to confront death. Chinese culture deals explicitly and effectively with this challenge: The aged are still revered (if less so than before), the aging process is valued and ritualized with key celebrations, death is an open affair, and the question of immortality is dealt with in a number of ways. In Taiwan and Hong Kong, the family is still pictured as an immortal vehicle that is present before the person is born and goes on after he dies. The person occupies a momentary place in its suprapersonal trajectory. In China, this cultural norm is a major covert value orientation in the society. In the rhetoric of Communism, however, another idiom has been used, until fairly recently, to articulate at least symbolic immortality: This is the idea of contributing personally to the building of a nation. For a few, it means being viewed as a revolutionary martyr and commemorated by the living in order to sacrifice for the nation. For those too secular and "red" to find solace in the covert idiom of family, there is much meaning to be seen in the idea of building a nation even through such minute tasks as polishing a steam engine, watching children in a day-care center, and taking care of patients.

Both in my psychotherapy with American patients who are unable to come to terms with aging and death and in my own personal development toward that eventual end, I have learned a great lesson from the Chinese about a truth central to all traditional cultures yet so easily lost amid the narcissistic images of modernism. The practical down-to-earth genius of Chinese culture makes everyone take note of death — regularly — as a "natural" part of life. Concern to make one's death live up to family and national ideals is inculcated in children. Death gives meaning to life, to everyday life, to each life.

112

REFERENCES

1. Lasch C: *The Culture of Narcissism.* New York, Harper Colophon, 1979.
2. Kleinman A: *Patients and Healers in the Context of Culture.* Berkeley, University of California Press, 1980.
3. Brown G, Harris T: *The Social Origins of Depression.* New York, Free Press, 1978.
4. Obeyesekere G: Depression, Buddhism and the works of culture, in Kleinman A, Good B (eds): *Culture and Depression.* Berkeley, University of California Press, 1985, Chap 4.
5. Shweder RA: Menstrual pollution, soul loss and the comparative study of emotions, in Kleinman A, Good B (eds): *Culture and Depression.* Berkeley, University of California Press, 1985, Chap 6.
6. Rosaldo M: *Knowledge and Passion.* Cambridge, University of Cambridge Press, 1980.
7. Geertz G: *Local Knowledge.* New York, Basic Books, 1983.
8. Levy R: *Tahitians: Mind and Experience in the Society Islands.* Chicago, University of Chicago Press, 1973.
9. Myers F: Emotions and the self. *Ethos* 1979; 7:343-370.
10. Marsella A, White G (eds): *Cultural Conceptions of Mental Health and Therapy.* Dordrecht, Holland, D Reidel Publishing Co, 1982.
11. Keyes C: The interpretive basis of depression, in Kleinman A, Good B (eds): *Culture and Depression.* Berkeley, University of California Press, 1985, Chap 5.

From 'CULTURE AS AUTOGNOSIS' to 'BACK TO MYSELF'

Dr Kleinman adds to our inventory of factors that enhance useful knowledge of ourselves and meaningful personal development. He brings to our attention society, culture, and environment in a special way and demonstrates that differences can be studied rather than rejected or papered over. He describes the dramatic contrast between the cultures familiar to him in America and in China and the resultant changes in his own thinking, personality, and life.

Dr Kleinman's report reverberates with Dr Rice's "Surprise." Even the less striking contrasts among the subcultures that we experience within our own country can increase our perspective and depth of understanding.

Some of the knowledge that he imparts to us reinforces concepts underlying forms of psychiatric treatment that have evolved in recent decades. The observation that "when we begin to change our external behavior in a systematic way supported by the culture around us, our inner experience begins to change" is close to the rationales for cognitive behavior therapy and for group therapy. The addition of meaningfulness to an individual life that derives from membership in a family is a strong factor in the effectiveness of family therapy. The malleability of personality that Dr Kleinman observed supports the broadened concepts of personal development that have expanded Freud's early ideas that personality was largely established in the first five years of life.

For our purposes, these supports for various therapies can be useful. One of the objectives of autognosis is to apply therapeutic methods to ourselves to bring about favorable and healthful changes.

In contrast to a culture in which the family is described as providing comfort, support, and meaning, the next essay presents almost the opposite. It presents a situation in which the family was experienced as a burden and a stress.

Chapter 21

BACK TO MYSELF

Louise Dierker, M.D.

It is the mid-1960s at a Midwestern university. It is spring and the shadows of late afternoon cross the courtyard of a three-story brick building. The building is part of the university's medical complex, built in the 1950s as part of the expansion of the medical school. It is the inpatient psychiatric facility, a referral center for a large portion of the state.

The darkness of a basement corridor, windowless, subterranean, contrasts with the bright green and light pastel colors of the spring landscape. Walking down the corridor is a quiet, sad, young woman rumpled and exhausted from a day's work on the medical wards. Her short, cropped hair and dark-rimmed glasses give her an edge of severity. The white, untailored medical jacket adds to this plainness, and conceals her femininity. She does not want to be seen by other medical personnel in that particular corridor. The young woman enters an office where an older male psychiatrist sits quietly waiting. The door closes.

As the psychiatrist speaks, gently inquiring about concerns, the medical student begins to talk. Her monotone voice reveals the grief she feels, and the clenched fist, the anger. The loss of her beloved within the month is told. And, after this, there is a torrent of words and tears. She describes her frustration, frustration at the inordinate demands of medical school, and the lack of understanding of her own family. Her parents rely on her to be available to

114

them, to be loyal, with no thought of her own grief or of the duties and workload of medical school. "The only support they give," she says, "is financial, and the expectation is that I therefore owe them constant support."

The psychiatrist listens and begins to form a picture of the situation. He gives the support she needs at this crucial time. Throughout the summer months and into the fall she continues weekly psychotherapy. The psychiatrist begins to help her see her part in these difficulties. With this growing awareness, she begins to solve the conflicts that have been causing her so much pain.

During these same months, the medical student begins a clerkship in psychiatry and is "the doctor" within the same building where she is an outpatient. She is assigned to the inpatient ward. The psychiatric clerkship is a new one for the whole medical school. This young woman is part of the first class to be required to take this clerkship. She approaches it with trepidation verging on terror, as she walks down the hall of the inpatient ward. Her hope is that her first patient will be a quiet depressed woman. The first patient admitted to the ward that day will be hers to follow. Suddenly, the ward attendants push open the door entering the ward and struggle to bring in an adolescent girl. The girl is screaming and thrashing as she is carried to the seclusion room. The medical student reacts with fear, fear of the patient's violence and fear of her own inability to handle the situation.

In the coming weeks throughout the summer months, the young woman patient and the young woman medical student confront each other. The patient improves and, at the end of the student's rotation, is discharged from the ward. The end of this rotation brings with it the requirement of a paper on the subject of the medical student's choice. The student chooses her patient, A., and writes a case report about her experiences in attempting to treat A.

7/2

What am I doing here standing against the wall of this small barren room looking at her? She is almost sexless, clad in the plain cotton pajamas, sprawled on the mat peering at me under the drooping eyelids. Her face shows only hardness, and there is no indication of response to my stilted introduction of myself. In fact, most of her attention is directed toward the mat, with intermittent movement of her hands to her head. Her eyes reveal fear, and her voice has the high-pitched timbre that makes me think she is going to cry, but she doesn't and the face is emotionless.

7/5

Today A.'s speech is very slurred and rapid, and she seems confused. She is more emphatic about her curly hair and loudly tells me how horrible it is to have curly hair. Her distress creates a feeling of sadness in me. She only looks at the floor, and I feel out of touch with her.

7/7

As I enter the four-bed ward, A., lying on her bed, turns away from me to face the wall. Her response to my hello is one of cold, sarcastic mockery. She emphatically expresses her anger about being given medications. I ask her how she is feeling. She bitterly replies, "Don't give me the third degree." Her hostility makes me angry and I feel the impulse to get up and leave, but I don't. We sit in silence; she looks at the wall and I gaze out the window. She tells me to quit looking at her, and I explain that I am not. Impatient with my silent presence and unwillingness to talk she says, "You can sit here and look at the wall with me as long as you like." For some reason the "with me" seems to jump out and creates a feeling of warmth in me. Maybe her verbal hostilities are her only means of communication. Perhaps there is hope.

7/9

A. sits reading in the dayroom as I approach her about talking to the attending physician. Her response to this is a forceful and curt "No!" I withdraw, feeling insecure about forcing the issue, and leave the room. The nurse wisely suggests that A. be told she must come. With this support, I then ask A. to come, this time letting her know there is no choice. Amazingly, she consents as long as I don't walk behind her. I amble toward the room where the interview is to occur, which is at the end of the corridor. A. follows ten feet behind, slowly shuffling in her slippers, glancing quickly from side to side over her upraised arms as if to ward of any attack from her flank. When I turn to see if she is following, she skitters into the nearest doorway and waits for me to turn and continue on. She is terrified she will be touched by me or other patients, and keeps an extreme distance. An eternity later, she scoots into the room and sits in the chair to face the interviewer. Her response to the interview is one of silent withdrawal. Surprisingly, she does not leave the room. Today A. won her battle with the hallway, and somehow the failure of the interview seems rather unimportant.

7/22

How should I answer A.'s question, which she prefaced with the demand that I be straightforward? Why is she here, or perhaps the question I seem to be struggling with is, how do I explain it to her? I feel frustration, as if I were in a foreign land battling in a language that is neither my own nor the patient's. Inside I am screaming, "Please, A., please see! Understand! Can't you see!" Oh, God, how helpless I am!

8/7

A.'s face looks soft and feminine today as she teases me. No hardness, no fear, and a glimmer of a twinkle in her eyes. Although her hair remains hidden under the white towel, she doesn't speak about it or fuss with it. We walk to the drinking fountain together, her arms remain at her side even when we go through the doorway together. I can put my hands on her bed, and when she hands me a book our fingers lightly touch. As I talk to A.'s older sister, the look of amazement and respect in her eyes when she speaks of A.'s improvement makes me happy. . . .

As the medical student struggles to finish the case report, she becomes aware of an intense anguish. The anguish is about the differences so obvious between the two of them; she is an outpatient, A. an inpatient. She could understand A.'s anger; she herself felt anger. She could understand A.'s fear; she herself felt fear. What are the reasons for these differences between them?

> I lost myself in the very properties of their minds: for the moment at least I actually became them, whoever they should be, so that when I detached myself from them at the end of a half-hour of intense concentration over some illness which was affecting them, it was as though I were reawakening from a sleep. For the moment I myself did not exist, nothing of myself affected me. As a consequence I came back to myself, as from any other sleep, rested.
>
> (*The Practice,* William Carlos Williams, M.D.)

It is now the early 1980s. In an Eastern city, a psychoanalyst listens. The patient, feeling vulnerable on the couch, speaks of her pain and confusion. To give up control and "self-sufficiency" so esteemed in this society, and to come for help, is so very difficult. The patient says, "How humiliating it is to come to you and reveal my problems. I must have this help, but how could you ever understand how humiliated I feel? You are an attractive woman, married with children. You have it all together."

It is one day later; another time, another hour, and another patient. The psychoanalyst listens as the young woman sitting before her says, with flushed face, how embarrassed she is that she cannot manage her own life. The young woman is dressed plainly and wears dark-framed glasses. She speaks of her desire to discover who she has been and who she is now. She has lost the ability to laugh and to enjoy the lightness of life.

As the young woman talks on about the details of her life, revealing the depth of her distress, the psychoanalyst fleetingly looks to the wall behind the patient. There on the wall are the degrees and certificates from various universities, including one dated from the mid-1960s from a Midwestern university. The emotions come back vividly to the analyst, as they are echoed by the young woman patient who sits before her. The psychoanalyst remembers her own first journey to a psychiatrist. On that beautiful spring day, the darkness of the basement corridor contrasted with the sunshine outdoors. It seemed then that the darkness of her need for psychiatric help labeled her as different from her peers in the medical school. She felt very alone, orphaned. It is the memory of her first walk into patienthood that sustains her. Having been there, having changed; having been there again, having changed; and having been there even again, and having changed again. She knows that others can do the same, for they are neither worse nor better.

She lives with the truth of her own patienthood as she searches with patients for the answers to the question, "Why?" Why does one event create a crisis and not another? Why do some seek help while others, under stress, do not? Why do some persons mature while others are paralyzed in the turmoil of their own making?

These questions, formed in childhood, verbalized with her first psychiatric patient, are ones she still asks in analytic work. The answers elude her, but in the process of searching, some are helped. That is enough.

---

om 'BACK TO MYSELF' to 'MID-LIFE RUMINATIONS'

"Back to Myself" indicates that deficiencies in nurturing and strengthening in one's own family may be replaced in a healing way through other relationships in the culture. The perceived kinship between patient and physician, in some instances, may replace—in part—the help that families are expected to provide.

In the previous essay, Dr Kleinman called attention to the emphasis on family support and structure in Chinese society. While the cultural supports for the famiy are not as pervasive and significant in America, other resources are sometimes available. Psychotherapeutic relationships can, to some extent, serve as alternatives or reinforcements in situations in which the family was insufficient.

"Back to Myself" focuses on the experience of a woman who became a medical student, a physician, and then a psychoanalyst. This is a fairly specific career path, but the essay suggests some generalizable processes for others. Educational and professional relationships can sometimes provide empathy and needed sense of kinship. What Dr Dierker adds to this observation is that such substitutions are best not attempted mindlessly. The similarities and differences need to be examined closely. Cognition must be added to intuition.

Another element that Dr Dierker calls to our attention is the awareness of the influence of time. She observes the similarities between herself as a medical student and the patient's past and present. She takes note of the changes in herself from the past to the present. Her recognition of the actuality of favorable change in her own life helps her to see its possibility in the life of her patient. Although she is unable to answer some of the profound questions that occur in her work, she recognizes that patients are helped. The importance of healing and comfort are reinforced by her own experience.

The significance of the passage of time and what it brings is a major consideration in the next essay, "Mid-life Ruminations." Whereas Dr Dierker emphasized the improvements in life that can come with time, Dr Joel Rubinstein calls our attention to some of the pain and limitation that accompany progress.

Chapter 22

MID-LIFE RUMINATIONS

Joel F. Rubinstein, M.D.

My arrival simultaneously at the age of 40 and the tenth anniversary of my clinical practice heightened my awareness of aging. The passing of the years has affected my therapeutic as well as personal attitudes. Sometimes I have to remind myself that I have known the person sitting across from me a long time; we have aged together, sharing in a strange kind of face-to-face intimacy, in 50-minute hours separated by days at a time. A stop-action camera would show a rapid metamorphosis, but my own experience of time passing is barely noticeable.

Since I began practicing as a psychiatrist, my father died in his late 50s and an ever-growing number of contemporaries have passed away. These losses remind me that although 50 minutes may at times seem like a lifetime, my patients' suffering is time limited, as is our work together. Lifespans are miniscule in the face of historical time. More important, the opportunity for change and the time available is short-lived. The old adages about "wasting one's own life" begin to take on meaning and poignancy, and I convey this to my patients. I confront them, "You don't want to live life wishing always that you had done it differently!" Or am I confronting myself?

In the face of stalemated life situations, people must either make a change or realize they are actively choosing a compromised situation as the lesser of evils. In order to support my patients' sense of choosing, interventions often take the form of reframing the

121

subject to stress the positive. The negative aspects of the situation are a major reason the patient comes for therapy. Recognition of the choice involved takes on a greater imperative when a lifetime is seen as limited. Otherwise old age and death catch one feeling like a victim and looking back with regret, thus negating consciously a lifetime.

Psychiatric training emphasized the notion of grieving as a necessary and healing affect. At that time, I thought mainly in terms of grieving childhood hurts and losses, those "good enough" developmental experiences that simply did not happen. On the other hand, the reality of repetitive and ongoing grief has become a part of my life as it does for everyone whose life is not cut short. Thus, patients who fear relationships because they may be lost are reminded that all relationships are eventually lost. Invariably, one person survives the other, even if the individuals are inseparable emotionally. Aloneness intrudes constantly. Sometimes, one's exposure to loss matches the ability to adjust, but the opposite is more likely.

I find myself able to cope in the sense that grief does not destroy my functioning or level of enjoyment, but the reservoir of feeling seems deepened or painfully enriched. My experience of loss and grief is available to share with my patients as actual tears or intense feelings of being with the other person. Often I can see myself in tears outside my father's hospital room. The sob in my chest has diminished, but the tears still well up.

I am often asked, "Why do I still feel awful?" to which I reply, "What else would you expect given how much you loved!"

Grief also intensifies my realization of professional helplessness. Physicians were unable to diagnose either my father's carcinoma even with surgical sections or my mother's acoustic neuroma. Both believed in the medical profession and sought the "best" practitioners in their urban community. My decade of clinical practice showed me how small the area is in which the therapist can hope to see change. Often the quality of life in only a small sphere can be improved. For example, auditory hallucinations may become more tolerable but not disappear, or a depression may be lifted in a month instead of six months, and I know that it will probably return within the year. A woman with a life devoted to caring for a child or a parent with whom she has always been overly enmeshed may need to learn that only you and she recognize the magnificence of her devotion. One should consider such a reframing instead of the conclusion that she is an infantile dependent person, a conclusion that devalues her contribution to others. In the last example, she may seek a complete overhaul of her life, but smaller goals must be accepted.

Often, one must only aim to bear unbearable wounds from the past. These lesions cannot be "worked through" and are not unconscious or born in conflict. The harshness of the environment cannot be denied. Raising children alone is a frightening prospect. The suicide of a loved one cannot be undone.

Some patients described as having personality disorders directly confront my helplessness and consequently my existence as a therapist. Working with numerous "difficult patients" over the decade has led to an earlier acknowledgement of this reality directly with these patients as they seek to devalue the therapy or idealize the therapist. Over time, my sense of what is possible becomes increasingly more realistic. Perhaps it can aid patients to achieve a more realistic sense of themselves. Patients come hoping to have problems solved and answers given just as they expect from other physicians. I offer participation in a mutual endeavor that is extremely expensive and whose results are uncertain at best. Willingness to buy such services speaks to the degree of despair experienced.

The years passing also seem to emphasize the repetitive quality of human interactions and the human condition. Having provided supervision in one milieu for seven years, I see the same issues arise repeatedly. The members of the staff have changed, but each new group seeks to find the "correct" solution to each problem. Yet, a consultant's viewpoint, with his different level of involvement, can highlight opposing arguments, which usually make their decisions compromise. For example, the staff must constantly balance rulemaking and control in their roles as therapists, administrators, and ensurers of the safety of the milieu with individual client freedom. Some staff groups make rules, and others use the milieu group to generate standards with a staff veto. Which solution is right, one wonders. There seems to be good reason to do or not to do either one. The staff milieu is made up of professionals with varied training. There is constant conflict between sharing responsibilities and recognizing individual skills. Seeing the same struggles on many occasions, I found that the ability of the staff to agree is often more important than the actual decision.

This same experience of working in a hospital milieu for many years has provided me with a historian's role as well. My chronic status (as well as that of some of the patients) makes me the bearer of the history of the milieu and its functioning. I am constantly surprised at the assumptions I make about how things will be done only to find that I do not share my history in the milieu with the staff. It is not that others disagree with me, but they simply have a different experience. They do not know what happened when various approaches were tried, when other staff left, or when the program lived in other places. I feel that without the input from new staff, the old history would lead to stagnation. Yet the view of "having seen it before" adds a stability and promise for the future.

The passing years also mean I have aged with some of my patients of many years. Some have come intermittently and others continuously. Most striking is the lack of recognition of the time passing. The relationship has a stability that binds one to time. Perhaps it's a transference phenomenon. However, there seems to be a part of us that denies the reality of time. Its passing is marked by meals, holidays, watches, and calendars, but feeling is not generated unless, perhaps, we have an endpoint ahead.

Childbearing or child rearing change to grandparenting, illness, and retirement. Couples who originally presented unable to agree about raising a child now struggle with living as a dyad. These changes take place with my presence as a factor, possibly a minor one. Often life events occur faster than personality change can yield better adjustments. The therapist becomes a companion of sorts through these turbulent events.

After many years with a patient, one wonders if the memory-experience of parent and child is repeated by therapist and patient.

What is the reality of selective memory? Do I remember my patient's history with me and in their lives the way they do? I find that I may have fallen behind in my awareness of their current issues as I associate to old patterns that I identified early in therapy. In addition, my life has changed bringing new experiences of parenting my own children, caring for a handicapped parent, running a business, and dealing with my own physical frailty among other things. Despite therapeutic "objectivity" I cannot help listening with my own experience to patients. To some extent, it is the sieve through which one strains the patient's material for patterns of maladjustment. Of course, many other factors come into the process as well. Empathy certainly changes with one's own experience and understanding of the context.

My patients are aware of my age as well as many other facets of myself and my practice, which I may or may not want to acknowledge. Those people I have known for a long time become aware of patterns in my life, such as vacation decisions. I experience the decision to vacation two weeks in the spring as a spontaneous plan made during the dregs of the New England winter. However, it is experienced as a predictable act by my veteran clients. I intend to discuss my leaving a month ahead of time, but they are reacting to it long before I present the fact. More subtle aspects of change in my routine are only too apparent. Levels of fatigue reflected in lack of patience, injuries such as a recent back strain resulting in the use of a cane — or elation from some other experience brought to the hour as general good humor — all impact on patients' perceptions. They may wonder if I am mad and planning to fire them (ironically, firing my employer) or am I falling apart physically or taking their problems too lightly?

The end of life and therapy is brought home by the death of patients from disease, accident, or suicide. Therapy deals with living and the quality of life. The sudden death of a patient, without good-byes, highlights the question of the meaning of therapy. Even when suicide is not involved, the death of a patient confronts me with grief once more and with the inner tears. There is no future for that person to work toward. Conflicts will never be resolved.

The period of time needed to enjoy whatever changes are possible from therapy is not available. What might have been will never be. Yet their suffering is also ended — to a degree our work could never have achieved.

Of all these premature terminations, suicide of a patient has been the most painful. When the answering service called to tell me that the coroner needed to talk to me about her death, the roar in my ears, the shaky knees, and the palpitations came immediately and stayed for days. She had been alone in the woods when strangers found her. My call to her parents was their first notification. Ten days later at a physicians' meeting, I found out that another patient I had evaluated for suicide was brought to the emergency room the previous week d.o.a. with a gunshot wound.

I know that suicide simply hastens an event that is already in the near future. Yet to the therapist the act seems to negate the work that is aimed at living. There are no good-byes, by unilateral choice, but suicidal good-byes are impossible in therapy. The suicidal thought may be an impulse that will pass. An attempted good-bye by the patient would require consideration of action on the therapist's part to provide for the patient's safety. Feelings of helplessness become overwhelming to the point that they must be denied. The denial leads to feelings of ineffectiveness and fantasies of leaving psychiatry. Somehow, I must grieve for my patient as well as for myself without despairing.

As a psychiatrist, I have always been aware that I was in the business of selling my time. Lots of this commodity has been delivered, and I realize that its distribution has had a profound effect on me and on my customers. Sometimes my brief therapeutic contacts, even if spread over many years, end in tragedy or at least bittersweet experiences. Yet the richness of the human experience despite all its sufferings constantly unfolds in my office and provides a never-ending source of wonder and growth.

rom 'MID-LIFE RUMINATIONS' to 'THE MIND-BODY PROBLEM'

Dr Rubinstein employs a precise time-sense to enlarge and deepen an understanding of his own life and the lives of his patients. He examines several temporal frames: the 50-minute therapy session, the months or years over which he has treated some of his patients, phases of his life as a whole, and historical time.

He traces emotions and actions in these temporal frames. As a competent psychotherapist, he looks at origins and at goals. He examines the current situation and tries to discover how the patient can proceed to the objective. He negotiates the goal to correspond with what is feasible, which is not always what is ideal.

He applies temporal review to himself, where he is, and how he arrived. He leaves us with his appreciation for the richness of professional experience and his human participation in it. We infer that he expects it to continue, and we can expect it, too.

The latter is an example of the reframing mentioned early in the essay, a reminder that choices are possible. It permits focusing on the constructive side of a situation even when the painful and tragic elements are clamoring for attention. Dr Rubinstein shows us how he can apply it in reviewing his own experience in a way comparable to that for patients. This is an autognostic intervention, a therapeutic method that one can apply inwardly.

Some of the richness emerges from Dr Rubinstein's skill in observing the fine points of experience: events and their associated images and feelings. Attunement to the details of life is one of the skills sought and developed by effective psychotherapists. It can enrich the lives of psychotherapists and others who develop awareness and attention.

In the next essay, too, Dr Albert V. Vogel demonstrates the significance of details.

Chapter 23

THE MIND-BODY PROBLEM

Albert V. Vogel, M.D.

Although it may be true that some such events occur with overwhelming impact, it is my experience that most life events contributing to self-knowledge do so by small increments. Experiences that are larger than everyday occurrences are more likely to be found in political slogans and romantic novels. If one waits for the great happening to manifest itself, one may very well miss the all important, less dramatic events that contribute most to self-awareness. The same principle applies in psychotherapy as well: Although we as therapists may fantasize about the magical, life-changing event or intervention that will bring about the well-being of our patient, in more sober moments it is clear that most therapeutic change occurs slowly, with units of change (be they behavioral or insight, or both) being rather small. This is not to deny that dramatic, large increments occur, nor to denigrate them when they do. Rather, I wish to emphasize the importance of smaller, more frequent events that in sum contribute the most to our understanding of ourselves as well as to therapeutic change in our patients.

To illustrate I will describe several, small events in my life that have promoted the development of my current understanding of the Cartesian mind-body problem. This problem, that of psychosomatics in the broadest sense, is of considerable importance to me in my work as a consultation-liaison psychiatrist. Most of my patients are seen in a general hospital setting. Although many patients are referred to me because their physicians believe that they have a "psychological rather than a physical problem," it has long since become clear that most patients have a combination of physical and psychological difficulties. Because of increasing interest and exposure in both the medical and lay literature, terms such as holism, psychosomatic, and mind-body have become trite, as has the mention of the classical Greek thinking on the subject. Nonetheless, in the clinical practice of psychiatry in a medical setting, physicians and patients alike frequently feel the labeling of a particular symptom as psychosomatic to be a slur. Patients and their physicians frequently fight over whether their problems are "only psychological." Patients with physical causes for their symptoms are considered to be ill and deserving of treatment, care, and perhaps financial compensation; physical problems, which are thought to have been caused or contributed to in some way by psychological factors, are seen as weakness. They are, in some way, not legitimate, perhaps not even considered illness.

A number of clinical experiences have brought this problem home to me. But, I sensed in myself a considerable tendency to agree secretly that physical symptoms with psychological determinants are somehow less worthy than pure somatic illness. The American tradition is "mind over body" not "mind and body." So, with the advent of biofeedback, relaxation, and other such techniques, there is no stigma to using mind to affect physical problems, for example, to lower blood pressure in an individual with hypertension. But it commonly remains a stigma or affront if the mind, without conscious control, contributes to dysfunction rather than to promoting better function. Those of us brought up in the tradition of the American West as portrayed in innumerable westerns have learned this. Imagine if John Wayne had a tension headache. Or what if he obtained a placebo-induced analgesia while undergoing one of his inevitable surgical bullet extractions.

Although many clinical experiences have contributed to understanding of psychosomatic events in me, and in general, I will describe two here. These have interacted with at least two personal experiences.

Not too long after beginning practice in a university hospital setting, I was asked to see Mrs A., a 32-year-old, married woman, because she had been discovered factitiously raising her temperature by rubbing the thermometer against the bedsheets. At this time, she was in her third hospitalization postpartum because of continued pelvic pain. About four months before, she had given birth to her second child, followed within a few days by an episode of endometritis treated with antibiotics. Although intermittent low-grade fever and pelvic pain persisted, the efforts undertaken so far had failed to reveal any cause for her continued symptoms. Her physicians were beginning to believe that the pain was in some way psychologically determined. The discovery of her manipulation of the thermometer was the last straw and convinced them that this was undoubtedly the case. In talking with me she explained that during the course of her four hospitalizations she had become aware that if she had a fever her physicians would take her complaints of pain seriously and would continue evaluating the problem. With each hospitalization, when her fever resolved she had been discharged home, only for the pain and then the fever to return. When this happened her physicians would have something objective and would rehospitalize her for further study. The thermometer episode came when she knew that she was physically ill and was about to be discharged again without treatment. So, to prevent this she provided her doctors with "objective" findings. Not long afterward, her fever returned without her assistance, and exploratory surgery revealed a large pelvic abscess. Drainage resolved all her symptoms.

This woman's experience raised a number of issues. In the presence of physical illness, as yet undiagnosed, psychological and interpersonal factors altered the presentation and course of her illness. She did it in a way that seemed reprehensible to her physicians. But what would I have done in such a situation, being convinced of physical illness but being unable to persuade my physicians? Of course, I told myself that as a physician I could argue symptoms, syndromes, and etiologies knowledgeably enough to convince them to continue the workup until the undoubted physical cause was uncovered. But suppose I could not. What if I were powerless and ignorant? My initial response was, of course, that I would be objective about any of my complaints. I would "tell it like it is" without embellishment. I would not even consider the possibility that I might manipulate the history given to a physican caring for me. Certainly not consciously. Much less unconsciously.

Not long afterward, I developed, for the first time, symptoms of allergy to airborne pollen: nasal congestion and cough, with minimal wheezing. I visited an allergist who prescribed appropriate medication and asked that I call him weekly for three or four weeks to advise him of my progress without the need to visit his office frequently. I did not think that my symptoms improved. I made several of these telephone calls to him in my wife's presence using the kitchen telephone. On hanging up after the call before I was to return for an office visit, my wife asked me whether I had noticed that when I was on the phone with the allergist, I coughed much more frequently and more noisily than I did at other times. My first reaction was rapid, angry denial. She was, of course, in the dangerous position of telling me my own business, as she is not a psychiatrist nor particularly interested in the psychosomatic process. Wisely, she let the matter drop. I stewed about it for weeks. Occasionally, when I was willing to admit that her observation might be valid, I was forced to recognize that I was certainly not doing it on purpose, that is, not consciously. Was I then producing, or at least exaggerating, a physical sign to influence my physician? To persuade him that his treatment was not successful? Then I recalled Mrs A. Should my wife be correct in her observation — and I was now beginning to believe that it was at least possible — perhaps I had an answer to my question of what I would do in Mrs A.'s position. Then, before long, another clinical situation arose.

A psychiatric consultation was requested for Mr B., a 45-year-old man. The consultation request stated that he "does not appear to really be sick because he vomits only when a nurse or doctor is in his room." On arriving to see him I found a jaundiced, seriously ill man. All evidence indicated that he was in alcohol-related liver failure and that he also had pancreatitis. He had every reason to be nauseated and to vomit. But what about the timing? I asked him, and he answered that his doctors found him to be a chronic alcoholic with a self-induced problem and did not consider him worthy of treatment nor legitimately ill. He did not enjoy vomiting, and since he was nauseated essentially all of the time, he knew that doctors and nurses were likely to consider vomiting a sign of real illness, and so, when medical personnel were in his room, it was easy for him to stop fighting it. Unfortunately, his medical caretakers noticed the pattern and interpreted it as feigning illness. He was, indeed, feigning something. But it was not illness. It was not the vomiting that was feigned, it was the nonvomiting. Of course, to consider the process feigning seems unreasonably adversarial and says more about those who claimed he was feigning than it does about him. And it all made me rather sad.

Shortly afterwards, I attended a concert of the local symphony orchestra. These issues and questions were on my mind. Or, at least they were triggered by the everyday behavior of the audience. The audience coughed and cleared their throats between movements and only rarely during the music itself. Now presumably, people did not cough during intermission without needing to do so. But then they must also have needed to cough during the music. But they did not cough during the music. Thus they, as with Mr B., demonstrated control over a physical symptom or sign. It seemed absurd to consider that they were being deceptive in some way by not coughing during the music or by doing so during the breaks. Which was the normal condition, then: to cough or to abstain? Under the usual conditions of a concert the question is irrelevant. However, because I was feeling accused of psychologically manipulating my symptom, also cough, and because I remembered Mr B. and Mrs A., I saw the events of the concert in a different light: Clearly some members of the audience had colds, the flu, bronchitis, or some other physical reason to cough, and yet social or psychological needs (such as courtesy to other concertgoers or embarassment at being disruptive during the music) could modify the presentation of the physical condition that caused the cough. Perhaps this does not seem like a particularly novel revelation. But, possibly, it is the nature of autognosis that insight important to oneself is just that, important primarily to oneself. It has impact on me out of proportion to what it has on other individuals. In fact, it may have been "discovered" a thousand times before. But now I have discovered it. What was the true condition of the people in the audience: to cough or not to cough? What was Mr B.'s real condition concerning his nausea: to vomit or not to vomit? Silly questions, yet I was aware that the sort of all-or-none, mind-or-body thinking that leads to this kind of question is what I encountered frequently in consultations in the general hospital. Commonly, physician or patient believes that the problem must be either a physical illness or a psychological one: either/or, but not some of each. And, there is a sort of contamination theory as well: If the illness is in any way affected by psychological factors, then the whole illness or process must be psychological. It reminds one of the older racist doctrine in the American South that a drop of "negro blood" could somehow contaminate a much larger proportion of "white blood." So, an individual with only a single black grandparent or even great-grandparent was legally, and socially, black. I was now becoming aware that I was not immune to this kind of thinking, at least not when it came to my own situation concerning mind and body. The possibility that I was altering the presentation of my symptoms or illness for psychological reasons, especially ones beyond my conscious control, did not sit well. The idea that unconscious processes were important in my psychological life was neither novel nor disturbing; it had been a subject of considerable and continuing inquiry during and after residency. But this, this involving the physical, seemed different to me, somehow more difficult to accept. It produced a gut response and considerable resistance to admitting its validity. Why was it so easy to find psychosomatic components in my patients but so difficult to accept them in myself? And then it occurred to me that this might be related to my selection of the subspecialty of consultation psychiatry or psychosomatics. Was I concentrating on discovering such psychosomatic "flaws" in others to avoid the recognition of them in myself?

Physicians are thought to manifest relatively large degrees of counterphobic phenomena concerning illness and the dependence associated with it. It goes something like this: I am not afraid of illness or being dependent on others. In fact, I am so not afraid of it that by being a physician I am going to rub shoulders with illness all the time, expose myself to the perils of illness, and I will take care of others who are dependent on me—but I will certainly not be ill or dependent myself.

It seemed then that I was working on a sort of subspecialty variant of this in myself in the psychosomatic arena. In my consultation practice, it was protective for me to find psychosomatic issues in others and for me to persuade patients and physicians alike that it was acceptable to have psychosomatic components to illness. Perhaps I could also persuade myself.

Subsequently, a number of other events, feelings, and historical remembrances fell into place. They were each relatively minor, but in sum they contributed significantly.

My father had never taken a sick day in 40 years of work. My mother was chronically well, "never even catching colds," until in her eighth decade. I too have a personal saying that I use with my family that drives them up the wall, "I don't believe in headaches." I suspect this has been a part of a campaign to persuade my wife and children that the proper emphasis is mind-over-body rather than mind-and-body. How did I feel when told that I had an allergy, one of those classic psychosomatic conditions? And, how did I feel on learning that my brother-in-law had asthma? Somehow it was not proper to have such an illness, or the tendency to such, in the family.

One of my major research interests lies in demonstrating that people can achieve a significant, physical placebo response even after being told that they are receiving placebo. It is as though I would like to show that everyone can have psychosomatic "weaknesses" even when he or she knows, intellectually, about mind-body interactions.

Looking at this issue in myself is not finished and never will be. Has it been helpful? I think so. I am working at being less evangelistic now about persuading my associates and the patients that they refer to me that psychosomatic issues are present, but that they are not a stigma. I see a bit more clearly the importance of such issues in the natural history of illness, including in myself. I think I no longer crusade on the matter: This enables me to see my patients' psychosomatic issues, or the absence as just that: their issues. And, in turn, I may be more helpful to them. Together we work on their mind-body problems rather than trying to keep the lid on mine. I continue my research interest in placebo. However, I might have learned something interesting and useful about placebo whatever my motivations for studying the phenomenon.

And, not least, I hope to stop irritating my family with comments about not believing in headaches.

From 'THE MIND-BODY PROBLEM' to 'THREE CASES'

With the clinician's attention to detail and the intellectual integrity of the philosopher, Dr Vogel followed a difficult path to meaningful new knowledge about himself. His curiosity and recognition of the significance of events in and around himself contributed to his insight.

The observation of his wife served as an important catalyst in this process. The mutative effect of her comment is comparable to the role that Dr Zisook's wife played in the resolution of the writing block. Even though the comment rankled, Dr Vogel listened well. It is tempting to reject, dismiss, or override an unpleasant observation. If the temptation can be withstood, progress toward increased insight may be accelerated.

Dr Vogel alluded to the culture of the hospital in which physical symptoms are respected and considered valid. Dr Arthur Kleinman's observations of Chinese culture revealed similar respect for physical illness. The psychological is repudiated. Dr Vogel shows us the tenacity of such attitudes, as he discovered himself.

The observation about the suppression of coughing by a concert audience points to the extent to which symptoms may be tailored to social expectations. Dr Vogel stated that good health was expected in the family from which he came. Sickness, as exemplified by headache, was disapproved.

His hard-earned self awareness was liberating and is continuing. It seems inevitable that his expanded understanding of the mind-body issue in himself will strengthen him as a clinician, as a scientist, and as a family man.

In "Three Cases," Dr John T. Carr reveals to us additional personal insights that derive from psychiatric experience. They are built upon intellectual integrity and emotional fortitude.

Chapter 24

THREE CASES

John T. Carr, M.D.

My experience in psychiatry has been responsible for many healthy changes that have taken place in me. I had not been comfortable with myself for a long time prior to starting my psychiatric residency. I had recognized in myself most of my adult life an intolerance to anything less than perfect. As time went on, my life to the outside world probably looked ideal. I was an achiever and everything eventually seemed to fall in place for me with persistence and work.

Every time I worked through some insight I became less and less satisfied with myself. There were many traumatic events and disturbing involvements. With each of these I usually discovered some truth about myself. They didn't all have the impact of a hammer but they were usually felt, and they provided dawning recognition that things weren't right with me.

I did not once entertain the idea of going to a therapist. What I did do was to decide to be a psychiatrist. While I was making the decision to pursue psychiatric training, it never dawned on my conscious mind that I was in fact looking for answers to my own neurotic turmoil. Once I got involved in my residency training, though, my fears, inhibitions, and vulnerabilities came into focus, and the truth of my intent became clearer. I let insights seep in, and they usually made their impact during or after a therapy session. Occasionally, I was unable to deal with the transferences and countertransferences, and in one situation therapy was impossible.

137

I have chosen three cases that had special impact on me. There are others, but these were revealing to me and in each case something was learned and growth achieved.

Case number one was probably my first difficult case after starting in private practice. W.S. was a professional man who picked my name out of the phone book. He wanted help with some problems he had relating to women. He was white, aged 36, respected in his profession, but he could only develop relationships with black women. He had had a number of sexual affairs with white women but none was substantial, and they were usually women that he was trying to degrade in some way.

From the beginning I felt uncomfortable with W.S., but I did not know why. At any rate I agreed to see him twice a week at 7:30 AM. After three or four weeks, I recognized the acuteness of my discomfort and sought out supervision. I engaged the chief of psychiatry at my hospital (and was a little uncomfortable about that) and saw him once a week. I didn't deal with my unease about this patient right away in my supervision but chose to address the treatment of the patient, which was basically psychoanalytic psychotherapy.

I grew more upset. I had stopped looking forward to his arrival in my office every Tuesday and Thursday morning. I even began to lose sleep over it. In my struggle to understand what was happening, I decided that I was probably reacting to some latent homosexual attraction to him and therein must lie my anxiety. It took me a couple of weeks to finally address this issue with my supervisor. To my utter surprise, he had divined my discomfort and had already guessed its cause. He was, however, surprised at my self-diagnosis of homosexual fear. He saw this as a way of disguising the real issue, competition with the patient.

This case had a great impact on me, and a lifetime of terribly disturbing incidents became ever so much clearer to me. My problem was in no sense related to homosexuality, although I was ready to believe anything rather than deal with the fact that I was terrified of dealing with someone who was more intelligent than I. I was fearful of being caught without an answer, not knowing something. My supervisor's clarification was like the lifting of a veil. I suddenly realized why, for example, I had always done poorly on examinations. Just the posing of a question, either oral or written, raised my anxiety so much that I couldn't come up with the answer even if I knew the material. I also realized that it very heavily related to maternal criticism and insistence that I perform up to her impossibly high standards.

Obviously, in the case of W.S. my anxiety came from the fact that first of all, he was considerably more intelligent than I, and second, I didn't have all the answers about this new profession I was in, and third, I didn't have all the answers that W.S. was seeking. I was totally unable to see that I didn't have to deal with this intelligence; we were talking about his relationships and his problems around them. In fact, I did know more than he did about what was going on with him. He was in my yard now.

It was also interesting to realize that W.S. had also divined my discomfort, and he was using his intelligence as a way of keeping me away. There was the typical power struggle of two obsessive people. After that realization, therapy went quite well. He was a patient for over a year and continued for another year and a half in another part of the country with an analyst I referred him to. I have heard from him on several occasions since, and he is functioning well. His bogged-down career has blossomed, and he is happily married with two children.

Concerning my choice of supervisor, I was a little distrustful; he was a political animal and not above changing facts to fit a situation. I was and continue to be grateful for his astuteness and welcomed his interpretation of the source of my anxiety, but my lack of trust was on the mark. A number of months later, when he apparently perceived me as a threat to his position, he told the chief of another department in the hospital that he "had to supervise me on a case recently." It was a terrible breach of manners and abuse of confidence (especially since I was paying him), and he used the situation to deprecate me for political advantage. Everything turned out well though. For a multitude of reasons he soon quit his job and moved to another city, and I was elected chief of psychiatry shortly thereafter.

The next case was a disaster. I had begun to feel more comfortable in my role as a psychotherapist and had enjoyed what I determined was a measure of success in my new profession. I had treated a number of difficult cases and was settling in quite nicely when into my office came a 42-year-old female school teacher (J.B.) who was experiencing problems with her marriage, her administrators at school, parents of her pupils, and her few friends. She was a very angry, autocratic, demanding woman. She was also frequently seductive, and when she was successful at coaxing some warmth from me, she would clearly get across the message that it wasn't enough. She would spend a whole hour complaining that things were going nowhere. She put me down constantly for being "a man" and at those times when she was being most harsh toward me, she would want assurance that I cared for her and would not abandon her.

I recognized this woman immediately. She was my mother. She was a carbon copy of my mother, with whom I have always had "an arm's distance relationship." My feeling was intense from the beginning, and I decided before the first session was over that I probably could not treat her and was going to have to refer her to another psychiatrist.

I did no such thing. When the hour ended, I gave her another appointment and then a third and a fourth even though I knew that for her own good (and mine) it was best to refer her to someone else. Furthermore, there was no chance of getting supervision at this time, which I would have enthusiastically embraced. I kept this poor lady coming back, and even when I recognized why I was keeping her on as a patient, I still couldn't bring the "therapy" to a close. It took me 17 sessions to bring her relationship with me to a halt. When it finally came, she left with all guns firing and refused my suggestions to continue treatment elsewhere even though she had been in agreement the week before. She did not pay me after the fifth visit, and I did not ask.

I wish I could say I made a quantum leap forward as a result of this case or that I was able to help this woman resolve some of her own issues. But it did not happen. As a matter of fact, the truce that existed between my mother and me then was disrupted and we had some very difficult times. She is 80 years old now, and we have, over the last four or five years, repaired some of our feelings. I have finally realized that she never could, and certainly never will, at her age and state of health, be able to understand how I felt about receiving almost daily beatings when I was a young child up until early adolescence or how I felt about being made to say "I love you" after a beating for some mild transgression.

Unfortunately, the poor patient got caught up in my own rage, anger, ambivalence, and guilt. She never did go to the psychiatrist with whom I arranged her therapy, and I have no knowledge of her whereabouts since then. I would like to add, however, that that case was an opening wedge in my being able to reassess my relationship with my mother. I'm sure it would have proceeded much more rapidly had I secured therapy for myself at this point, but I didn't. I have let go of much of the anger and mistrust but have yet a ways to go.

It was a little painful recalling that case to mind again. It was seven years ago, and fortunately I have not had a recurrence of that situation. I have interviewed patients since then with whom I knew intuitively that therapy would go poorly and would be too taxing for me. I have declined them at the outset. That particular case was, without question, the most difficult situation I have been in as a therapist. I have been in a number of emotionally laden situations, but none as wrenching as that one.

The last case is of a 32-year-old wife of a naval officer (L.S.). She came to see me because of a succession of affairs when her husband was at sea (and sometimes when he wasn't). She was very attractive, quite verbal, expressed herself easily, and was remorseful over her infidelity. In the beginning, therapy went quite well. She was intelligent and psychologically minded. She was enthusiastic and I liked her. I didn't notice (or chose not to notice) that she was giving an increasing number of signs that she liked me and was attracted to me. I rationalized giving her the last appointment of the day. I didn't deal with the obvious pleasure I felt when Thursdays rolled around. I rationalized other little courtesies I extended to her. However, the time came when I could not rationalize my reactions.

I went for several weeks knowing that I had better address these feelings, which were obvious at this point, and of course her feelings were clear at this time also. She was very near to her moment of triumph.

To my everlasting satisfaction, integrity conquered desire and I exposed the whole charade. The next few weeks in therapy were painful but exciting — exciting in the sense that my integrity and morals were intact and her progress and understanding of herself unfolded and matured.

My own maturity as a therapist was immeasurably enhanced. She was in therapy almost six months after that, and it stands as a milestone in my career as a therapist. There have been several similar patients since, but fortunately I have been cognizant of the warning signs and have avoided similar experiences.

At the time I was treating this patient, my own marriage was beginning to disintegrate. This was in no small measure particularly responsible for my blindness. I can remember fantasizing that she could take my wife's place and that I would certainly be all that she would ever need in a man. In retrospect, I was also looking for an immediate replacement for my wife because of my fear of being alone.

I guess I should end by filling you in on what is currently going on with me. My immediate position in life is that of a successful psychiatrist in a small community. I am now divorced and happy to be out of that turmoil. My dependency needs are getting roughed up a bit but are subsiding to a point of manageability. I have felt sorry for myself frequently and angry with my ex-wife often for destroying my fantasy. But my life is reasonably pleasant and will get better.

All of my therapy experiences have helped me decide on the new, "hopefully final," direction that I want my career to take. I am developing a 48-bed alcohol treatment facility, which should be in operation in 10 to 12 months.

I now realize that I do not have the patience for long-term therapy. I have not sufficiently resolved a multitude of issues in a way that would make me a really effective therapist. However, all is not lost. I have been a teacher, a family practitioner, and a psychiatrist, and these lend themselves very well to a career in the treatment of alcoholics. For the last three years, my interests have moved toward crisis intervention, psychopharmacology, and alcoholism. And this is fine with me. I think I know how I got here.

HE LESSONS OF 'THREE CASES'

Dr Carr's life was stormy from the beginning, but instead of foundering, he managed to emerge with new insight.

He described himself as an "achiever" in terms of his appearance to the outside world. From our point of view, perhaps his greatest achievement is his ability to confront difficult situations and his contribution to them, to solve problems, and then to enhance his personal development. Like Drs Vogel and Armentano, he preferred to be the doctor rather than the patient. He indicates that this is one of the ways that he developed mastery over his own needs for help.

In his three cases he demonstrates how significant the therapist's subjective experience can be in the outcome of treatment. They also illustrate the autognostic benefit that can be gained by the therapist who is courageous enough to face frailties and vulnerabilities. It can protect patients from further harm and can promote their gains from treatment.

Dr Carr gained substantial benefit from inner searches. They led him to view his experience in terms of progress through life and increasing self-development. A major reward is a respect for his own skill to derive meaning, sustenance, and increasing strength from his experience. He developed it through raw courage and pain. It led him to a profound sense of how he got where he is, and to his hard-won confidence about the future.

Afterword

The autognostic studies presented in these essays were triggered by emotionally significant events. The precipitants were, in most instances, stressful and painful. They aroused the authors' attention and curiosity and were examined rather than avoided. The authors came to grips with the challenges; overcame nearly all; and in most, gained strength. Usually they derived benefit for themselves from the experience and, in the majority, extended its value to profit their patients or their own families.

Many of these essays dealt with events not peculiar to psychiatrists. Several were precipitated by events related to the authors' profession, but not specifically by patients. Many of the essays involved experiences related to work with patients. The confidence of these psychiatrists, as they face the future, is based on learning from errors and emotional storms. In this respect, they are like all of us.